Amtrak's Long-Distance Service
Can It Be Made Viable?

by
Gordon Gill

DORRANCE PUBLISHING CO., INC.
PITTSBURGH, PENNSYLVANIA 15222

All Rights Reserved
Copyright © 1998 by Gordon Gill
No part of this book may be reproduced or transmitted
in any form or by any means, electronic or mechanical,
including photocopying, recording, or by any information
storage and retrieval system without permission in
writing from the publisher

ISBN # 0-8059-4395-1
Printed in the United States of America

First Printing

For information or to order additional books, please write:
Dorrance Publishing Co., Inc.
643 Smithfield Street
Pittsburgh, Pennsylvania 15222
U.S.A.

Dedication

To all the railway passenger traffic officers and their staffs who have toiled through the years to offer a respectable transportation service.

"There ain't nothing more to write about, and I am rotten glad of it, because if I'd a knowed what a trouble it was to make a book I wouldn't a tackled it and ain't agoing to no more."

—Mark Twain, *Adventures of Huckleberry Finn*

Contents

Preface viii
Acknowledgments x
Chapter I. Economic Studies of Pre-Amtrak Rail Passenger Service 1
    1. Rock Island Railway Passenger Traffic (J.W. Kendrick, 1915)..............1
    2. Operating Expenses of the Rail Diesel Car 3
       (Coverdale & Colpitts, 1952)
    3. Railroad Passenger Deficit 4
       (National Association of Railroad & Utility Commissioners, 1952-58)
    4. Passenger Deficit Study (John E. Hansbury, 1953)................................8
    5. Railroad Passenger Service Costs and Financial Results 10
       (Stanley Berge, 1956)
    6. Cost Data for Railroad Passenger Service 12
       (Dwight R. Ladd, 1957)
    7. Passenger Train Costs (Aeronautical Research Foundation, 1957) ...14
    8. Passengers and Profit (Railway Progress Institute, 1959) 16
    9. Railroad Passenger Train Deficit (Interstate Commerce 19
       Commission, 1959)
    10. Railroad Passenger Traffic in the West 22
       (Stanford Research Institute, 1966)
    11. Intercity Rail Passenger Service 24
       (Interstate Commerce Commission, 1968)
    12. Investigation of Costs of Intercity Rail Passenger Service 27
       (Interstate Commerce Commission, 1969)
Chapter II. The Amtrak Era: Transition and Postimplementation Studies 30
    1. Basic National Rail Passenger System...30
       (U.S. Department of Transportation, 1971)
    2. Reports on Amtrak to the President and Congress 33
       (Interstate Commerce Commission, 1971 ff.)
    3. Reports to Congress on the Rail Passenger Service Act 36
       (U.S. Department of Transportation, 1973 ff.)
    4. Adequacy of Intercity Rail Passenger Service 38
       (Interstate Commerce Commission, 1973-76)
    5. Reports of Special Subcommittee 41
       (House of Representatives, 1974-75)
         A. The Blue Ridge 41
         B. The National Limited 43
         C. The Inter-American 44
    6. Report to Congress on the Amtrak Route System 46
       (U.S. Department of Transportation, 1979)
    7. Evaluation of Service to Areas Not Presently Served 50
       (Amtrak, 1992)

Chapter III. How Do Amtrak's Competitors Measure Up? 53
   1. Highway Travel 53
      A. Limitations Arising from Congestion 53
      B. Reductions in Safety 56
      C. Noise Abatement Contrivances 56
      D. Bus Alternatives 57
   2. Air Travel 58
      A. Public Costs and Subsidies 59
      B. Carrier Entry and Withdrawal from Markets 62
      C. Beneficiaries and Nonbeneficiaries of Air Carrier Deregulation 63
      D. Adverse Effects of Noise 64
      E. Weather-Induced Delays 66
      F. Matters of Safety 67
      G. Medical Considerations 69
      H. What Commercial Air Travelers Can Expect These Days 70
Chapter IV. Amtrak's Critics: Are Their Arguments Valid? 74
   1. Amtrak Yesterday, Today, and Tomorrow 74
     (Continental Trailways, Inc., 1976)
      A. Level of Amtrak Subsidy 74
      B. Cohesiveness of Rail Network 75
      C. Effect of Length of Rail Haul upon Losses 75
      D. Intermodal Competition 76
      E. Amtrak Fare Level 77
   2. Amtrak: An Experiment in Rail Service (Frank P. Mulvey, 1978) ... 77
      A. Safety 77
      B. Energy 78
      C. Environment 79
      D. Summary 80
   3. Amtrak: The National Railroad Passenger Corp. 81
     (George W. Hilton, 1980)
      A. Demand Conditions 81
      B. Cost Conditions 83
   4. United States Senators (1985) 85
   5. Miscellaneous Newspaper "Op-Ed" Articles (1985-95) 87
Chapter V. Amtrak's Missed Opportunities 89
Chapter VI. Evaluating the Demand for Rail Passenger Service 98
Chapter VII. A Proposed Amtrak Network 103
   1. New York/Boston-Chicago 104
   2. New York/Washington/Pittsburgh-Cleveland/Chicago 105
   3. Washington-Montréal/Niagara Falls 106
   4. Cleveland/Detroit-Cincinnati 106
   5. Chicago-Detroit/Pontiac 106
   6. Cincinnati-Chicago/St. Louis 106
   7. New York-Miami/Tampa 107
   8. New York-Cincinnati/Birmingham/Montgomery 107

9. Cincinnati/Jacksonville-New Orleans 107
10. Chicago-Jacksonville 108
11. Little Rock-Atlanta 108
12. Chicago-St. Louis/New Orleans 108
13. Chicago-Winnipeg/Seattle 108
14. St. Louis/St. Paul-Kansas City/Omaha 109
15. Chicago-Denver/Fort Worth/Albuquerque/El Paso 109
16. Denver/Albuquerque-Portland/Sacramento/Los Angeles 110
17. St. Louis-Fort Worth/Houston/San Antonio 110
18. New Orleans-Los Angeles 111
19. Seattle-Sacramento 111
20. Oakland/Sacramento-Los Angeles 112
Postscript on the Twenty Route Descriptions 112
Chapter VIII. Procedure for Ascertaining Revenues and Costs 115
Chapter IX. Where Do We Go from Here? 126
Appendix A—Proposed Long-Distance Network Timetables 132
Timetable 1 New York/Boston-Chicago 133
Timetable 2 New York/Washington/Pittsburgh-Cleveland/Chicago 134
Timetable 3 Washington-Montréal/Niagara Falls 135
Timetable 4 Cleveland/Detroit-Cincinnati 136
Timetable 5 Chicago-Detroit/Pontiac 137
Timetable 6 Cincinnati-Chicago/St. Louis 138
Timetable 7 New York-Miami/Tampa 139
Timetable 8 New York-Cincinnati/Birmingham/Montgomery 140
Timetable 9 Cincinnati/Jacksonville-New Orleans 141
Timetable 10 Chicago-Jacksonville 142
Timetable 11 Little Rock-Atlanta 143
Timetable 12 Chicago-St. Louis/New Orleans 144
Timetable 13 Chicago-Winnipeg/Seattle 145
Timetable 14 St. Louis/St. Paul-Kansas City/Omaha 146
Timetable 15 Chicago-Denver/Fort Worth/Albuquerque/El Paso ... 147
Timetable 16 Denver/Albuquerque-Portland/Sacramento/L. A. ... 148
Timetable 17 St. Louis-Fort Worth/Houston/San Antonio 149
Timetable 18 New Orleans-Los Angeles 150
Timetable 19 Seattle-Sacramento 151
Timetable 20 Oakland/Sacramento-Los Angeles 152
Appendix B—Overview of Foreign Rail Alternatives for Tourists 153
1. Europe 153
2. Asia 156
3. Africa 158
4. South America 159
Afterword 161
Postscript 166
Index 167

Preface

One of the author's earliest exposures to rail passenger service occurred while working during a college semester break as a freight handler at the former Camden Warehouses, adjacent to Camden Station in Baltimore, Maryland. (Then owned by the Baltimore and Ohio Railroad, the warehouse buildings are now part of Oriole Park at Camden Yards, home of the Baltimore Orioles baseball team.) It was possible to observe the periodic arrivals and departures of B&O's various passenger trains running between Jersey City, B&O's New York terminal, and the Midwest.

At the time, the author did not fully appreciate the interrelationship between such trains and others operated by connecting rail carriers at Chicago, St. Louis, Cincinnati, Detroit, and other points. But in due course, partly as a result of subsequent employment in a Class I railroad finance department, the "big picture" became apparent.

For a period of several decades, the author has observed the many changes that have occurred in this business, including the 1971 start-up of the National Railroad Passenger Corporation (Amtrak). Largely because of its continuing reliance upon U.S. Government subsidy, Amtrak's proper transportation role has long been controversial. Indeed, there is still today no consensus on how to structure the passenger carrier's future.

A number of writers have produced books addressing the corporation's history. However, to this author's knowledge, there is no extant book comprising (1) an examination of the myriad scholarly studies devoted to rail passenger economics undertaken before and after the inception of Amtrak; (2) an analysis of the shortcomings of Amtrak's highway and airway competitors; (3) a critique of other writers' evaluations of Amtrak's worth to the nation; (4) an assessment of Amtrak's market penetration deficiencies; (5) a survey of selected markets suitable for intercity rail passenger service; and (6) a plan for a national route structure, together with calculations of the associated costs, that provides societal benefits sufficient to justify a reasonable level of government assistance.

This book is intended to fill that void. It is hoped that the content herein, written as Amtrak begins its second quarter-century, is useful to policy-makers in their reexamination of the nation's economic priorities at a time when public expenditures of all kinds are increasingly open to scrutiny.

The text is directed to a nationwide readership and, hence, concentrates upon long-distance operations. Accordingly, it does not give consideration to high-frequency corridor service or certain stub-end regional or commuter trains sponsored by local governments. Also omitted from the book are analyses of such specialized services as Amtrak's Auto Train.

Finally, let it be explained at the outset what this volume is not. In no sense does it purport to present large quantities of statistical information. There are many publications, from government records to Amtrak's annual reports, that already contain these data. It is not a corporate history, although references to significant legislative turning points and strategic planning decisions unavoidably comprise an integral part. Neither is it a travelogue or compendium of Amtrak journey highlights; the author will leave such pleasantries to other writers.

—Gordon Gill

Acknowledgments

The author wishes to thank various acquaintances, both business and personal, who read portions or all of the manuscript and made valuable suggestions: Allan Baer, a long-time member of the CSX Corporation headquarters staff (and B&O Railroad before that), offered insightful counsel on little-known facets of many of the routes discussed herein.

Joseph Heberle and Robert Hasek, former associates of the author on the cost analysis staff at the Interstate Commerce Commission, spotted a few early flaws that otherwise might have remained undetected. Paul Graham of the compliance and enforcement staff made available railroad maps and employee timetables and provided general technical advice on operations. Albert West, chief librarian, unearthed a number of essential reference documents.

James Trousdale, career railroad industry employee (Missouri Pacific, Amtrak, North American Expediting Company), shared the wisdom gained during his long association with the business.

James Freeh, trusted friend and neighbor, helped in assuring that the document possesses general readability and clarity.

Dorsey Richardson, a travel agent based in Washington, D.C., furnished the author with countless rail tickets over the years and told fascinating stories from his own train travels (domestic and foreign) that inspired some of the content herein.

Elizabeth Reveal, Amtrak's former chief financial officer, and Tim Slottow of the corporate finance staff kindly furnished key operating statistics used in devising the *pro forma* projections.

Lastly, I must thank my wife, Linda, for her loyal companionship on trips taken to research the subject matter and for her understanding and support when my writing of the text sometimes extended well beyond the midnight hour.

—Gordon Gill

Chapter I
Economic Studies of Pre-Amtrak Rail Passenger Service

Readers may fairly ask why a book inspired by the continuing controversy over Amtrak's role in the national transportation network would include discussions of past economic studies. This author's response is that many of the issues now being debated are similar in nature (some of them very much so, as we shall see) to questions addressed by economists in earlier years. To the extent these analyses—presented here in sequential order—can help us comprehend the implications of any shift in transport policy that this country may be inclined to pursue, we stand to benefit from reviewing the existing body of knowledge. Some would call it "institutional memory."

1. Rock Island Railway Passenger Traffic (J.W. Kendrick, 1915)

[This subchapter is based upon the passenger traffic section of an analytical document titled *A Report Upon the Chicago, Rock Island & Pacific Railway* (referred to hereinafter as CRIP). Author Kendrick was not identified in 1915 editions of *The Official Guide of the Railways* as a CRIP officer. We might conjecture that he was associated with the securities industry because on page 241 of the document there is a reference to the "interest manifested by investors." To dispel confusion, we should note that in more recent times (before CRIP was dissolved as an independent carrier), the company was known as "Railroad," rather than "Railway," as in 1915.]

This document observed that although CRIP connected many important commercial centers, the carrier was facing intensive competition from other railroads paralleling most of its main routes. Nevertheless, it fought aggressively for available through traffic and, in doing so, ran over half its train-miles in passenger service, proportionately greater than other western railroads.

In recognition that such a high percentage was more than a byproduct of freight and in view of the company's overall passenger deficit, the document strongly suggested an increase in fares sufficient to permit recovery of all costs, direct and indirect. It also recommended that vigorous studies of revenues and expenditures be undertaken, with the goal of eliminating trains found incapable of contributing to net income.

Unfortunately (from CRIP's standpoint), to encourage traffic growth, eight of the fourteen states in which the carrier operated had imposed maximum fares of two cents per passenger-mile. Thereafter, the number of local passengers carried grew markedly, as the states intended. To have such maxima overturned in court, railroads bore the burden of demonstrating that the low fares were "confiscatory."

At the same time, CRIP's ability to interchange the more remunerative long-haul passengers with connections was limited. For example, the Gould lines (Missouri Pacific, Denver and Rio Grande Western, Western Pacific), which operated a complete transcontinental service of their own, garnered most of the passengers moving through the Colorado gateways. As to the El Paso route, connecting line Southern Pacific (SP) preferred to work with other carriers awarding it a longer haul.

The document further noted that some railroads had accustomed the public to luxury travel standards, notably through provision of observation cars with rear-platform viewing such as those popularized by Northern Pacific for operation over three scenic mountain ranges. However, since these cars were deemed less suitable in CRIP's primarily agricultural territory, it was recommended that the company not add such costly equipment to its fleet.

Citing a ruling by the Interstate Commerce Commission (ICC) in *The Five Per Cent Case*, 31 I.C.C. 351, 392 (1914), and various judicial holdings that railroads are entitled to a legitimate return on their investment and that freight shippers should not be expected to subsidize passengers, most of the industry initiated an effort to raise fares to three cents per passenger-mile.[1] Applications to regulatory bodies for intra- and interstate increases were accompanied by supporting cost analyses. These studies accounted both for direct passenger expenses and for the passenger portion of expenses common to the freight service. Separation of such common expenses between passenger and freight was initially based upon an 1890 method devised by the James J. Hill lines and, after July 1915, by ICC-prescribed rules. (See *In re Separation of Operating Expenses*, 30 I.C.C. 676 (1914).)[2]

---

[1] Later on, the Commission—citing changes in both statutory law and economic conditions—seemed to back away from this position. *Revenues in Western District*, 113 I.C.C. 3, 22-23 (1926).

[2] There have been other reports on this subject. See, for example, *Separation of Operating Expenses, Freight and Passenger*, 302 I.C.C. 735 (1958).

A breakthrough for the railroads occurred in Arkansas, where a federal district court lifted the two cents per passenger-mile holddown previously ordered by that state's Public Service Commission. However, CRIP passenger service as a whole remained in a deficit position.

The document stated that CRIP's traffic department should be restrained from establishing unremunerative fares published solely to meet competition from other railroads. An example was offered of fares for travel to expositions at San Francisco and San Diego that were set at about one cent per passenger-mile.

In a company study of September 1915 operations, expenses/fixed charges and revenues were calculated separately for fifty-seven CRIP main-line passenger trains. As a result of indicated losses, the railroad created and implemented a plan to scale back its service.

It is noteworthy that the Golden State Limited,[3] a superior train operating between Chicago and Tucumcari, New Mexico (en route to and from California via SP), was causing greater losses than some less known trains. The reasons included larger promotional expense, and—because of its fast schedule—cost of delay to opposing trains sidetracked for it, as well as a need for both heavier locomotives and greater track maintenance.[4]

With regard to CRIP's secondary trains, the document counseled exploring use of a new type of motor car then being produced by General Electric Company. The car reportedly had enabled the Ann Arbor Railroad to provide a profitable light density service. Some fear was expressed, however, that such cars might prove so attractive to passengers that they would generate loads beyond their seating capacity.

2. Operating Expenses of the Rail Diesel Car (Coverdale & Colpitts, 1952)

Pursuant to a 1949 request by The Budd Company, a manufacturer of railroad equipment, the New York-based consulting engineering firm of Coverdale & Colpitts (C&C) helped estimate operating and capital costs of

---

[3] Interestingly, the 1915 Golden State Limited bore the train numbers 3 and 4, identical with those still used in the last years of service (when the train was called simply the Golden State), about a decade before Amtrak. According to the *Official Guide*, the 1915 schedule was slower, however. For example, in that year the westbound train departed Chicago at 8:05 P.M.; through cars (characterized as "steel" and "electric-lighted") arrived on SP in Los Angeles three days later at 2:30 P.M. and in San Francisco the following morning at 8:50 A.M. On portions of the route, it carried St. Louis-Santa Barbara and Minneapolis-Los Angeles cars. In the 1950s, this train departed Chicago at 1:10 P.M. and arrived Los Angeles at 7:30 A.M. on the third day. Before final discontinuance, it was consolidated with SP's Sunset Limited west of El Paso.

[4] The opposite conclusion, however, is suggested in a 1948 study of well known "name trains." See subchapter 5.

a new style of self-propelled rail diesel car (RDC) then under development. The car was designed for use in a variety of services, ranging from short-haul suburban to long-haul intercity. Powered by two engines with torque-converter drives directly connected to one axle of each truck, it provided a high rate of acceleration. Capable of multiple-unit operation, the car was fitted with controls at both ends and was offered with optional baggage compartment.

In 1952, by which time seventy-eight of the cars had been sold and placed into service, C&C made a detailed cost study reflecting actual experience. Excluding cars used in "extreme" assignments, the firm identified fifty-four cars on fifteen U.S. runs comprising a mixture of one, two, and three-car operations. On average, these runs each generated about 73,000 miles per year.

C&C segregated the RDC costs by category: fuel, repairs (including allowance for general overhaul), crew, miscellaneous (lubricants, train and engine-house supplies, payroll additives), and fixed (insurance, depreciation, interest on investment). The average total cost per car-mile for the fifteen runs was calculated at 79.6 cents (mid-1952 price level).[5]

According to C&C, carrier personnel on all levels were pleased with the RDC. However, until certain corrections were made, either in the cars themselves or in track circuits, some difficulty was encountered relative to functioning of automatic signal devices. With regard to reliability, one railroad disclosed that no car had missed a scheduled run in over a year; others reported availability over 95 percent.

3. Railroad Passenger Deficit (National Association of Railroad & Utility Commissioners, 1952-58)

The National Association of Railroad and Utilities Commissioners or NARUC [now the National Association of Regulatory Utility Commissioners], an organization of state regulators, had traditionally monitored major facets of the railroad industry. In the late 1940s, this group began focusing more closely upon railroad passenger service

---

[5] The subject of RDC economics has appeared in the popular press. For example, *Business World* (Oct. 22, 1949, page 22) and *Popular Science* (December 1949, pages 114-117) describe a study which found RDC operating costs per mile to have then been 55 cents and 64 cents for two- and three-man crews, respectively. By contrast, the cost for a two-car steam train was $1.80 per mile. Also, see subchapter 5 for a reference to another C&C study covering costs of passenger trains using conventional equipment.

While Amtrak initially included some RDC equipment in its fleet and has experimented with other types of self-propelled cars, the concept apparently is not in favor today. Indeed, a successor to the RDC (known as the SPV-2000, also manufactured by Budd) never achieved wide popularity, although it was sold abroad, *e.g.*, in Morocco.

economics after commodity shippers stepped up their complaints that freight rates were set at an artificially high level to subsidize passenger deficits.[6]

Pursuant to the expressed concern, NARUC adopted a resolution in 1949 creating a committee to study the situation. Although it sought cooperation of the Interstate Commerce Commission (ICC) in this endeavor, the federal agency never budgeted specific funds therefor. The committee's various status reports, issued periodically over the next several years, form the basis for this subchapter.

A major area of interest involved the railroads' competition with air carriers. Of particular concern were the direct and indirect subsidies awarded these carriers through federal payments for transporting mail based upon a formula guaranteeing a profit, irrespective of the cost of service; provision of federally financed airways and other navigational facilities; use of airports at nominal charge; and leasing of military aircraft to private operators at a low rate of $300 per month, compared with $9,000 generally charged within the private sector. The railroads were further disadvantaged by legal mandates that they maintain capacity for handling mail, whereas air carriers were allowed to solicit the movement of mail on a space-available basis.[7]

Moreover, the failure of many states to assess adequate highway user charges against truck and bus operators was viewed as enabling the railroads' surface competitors to gain unfair advantage.

Additionally, the committee deplored continuation of the World War II-era 15 percent transportation tax, originally levied to discourage common carrier travel at a time when the rail infrastructure was overburdened. Requiring the carriers to collect and process the tax was seen as unwarrantedly adding to their clerical and accounting expenses.

The committee asserted that the Department of Defense should have been placing greater emphasis upon rail in transporting military personnel. Routinely moving troops by train would help justify retention in service of car equipment that may be needed on short notice in the event of war. Seven hundred sleeping cars, leased and held in reserve for emergency use, were believed insufficient in light of an independent

---

[6] The Interstate Commerce Commission had then recently granted the railroads general freight rate increases (*Ex Parte* Nos. 162 and 166) averaging 17.6 percent and 22.6 percent, respectively, and had pending before it a third increase (*Ex Parte* No. 168) estimated to aggregate more than a billion dollars annually.

[7] Courts have upheld the right of the Post Office Department to make experimental use of carriers other than railroads for transporting mail. See *Atchison, Topeka and Santa Fe Railway Company v. Summerfield*, 128 F. Supp. 266 (1955), 229 F. 2d 777 (1955), 351 U.S. 926 (1956).

government study concluding that 2,500 such cars were required to maintain wartime movement capacity.[8]

Further, the committee urged that state statutes be amended to eliminate arbitrary minimum crew manning standards, consistent with safe and efficient operation. Similarly, it regarded as "self-destructive" labor union insistence that management continue to assign firemen to modern locomotives not requiring their traditional skills and to compensate crews on a dual time-and-mileage basis incorporating an obsolete average speed equivalency factor.

The committee stressed a need for minimizing losses with respect to passenger-train handling of express shipments for the Railway Express Agency, jointly owned by sixty-eight railroads, which was then under extreme competitive pressure from noncompensatory parcel post rates. It also noted that recent rate increases granted by the ICC for transporting mail in passenger service should prove beneficial, although some diversion to truck could be expected. Revenues from hauling milk and cream were believed especially vulnerable to truck competition.[9]

Additionally, the committee criticized the carriers' service in some respects. Identified shortcomings involved air conditioning failures; a tendency to operate longer trains, thus relegating passengers to excessive walking along platforms; late-running trains; introduction of station porter charges, an outgrowth of new minimum wages imposed under the Fair Labor Standards Act; dining car prices regarded by some passengers as unreasonably high; maintenance of a locomotive weight basis for engineer pay, thus discouraging acquisition of more powerful locomotives; and employee discourtesy.

The committee did, however, commend the carriers in certain areas. These included the ordering of new, advanced-design equipment; accelerating replacement of steam locomotives with more economical diesel power; installing reclining seats in older coaches; rebuilding open-section sleeping cars with room accommodations; experimenting with fare levels by introducing thrifty family plans; and inaugurating electronic reservations equipment. While praising the advertising of passenger service in the print media, the committee believed the "full page spread of a sleek streamliner" also benefits freight service, such that the latter should be expected to bear a portion of the promotional expense incurred.

---

[8] *In Railroad Passenger Train Deficit*, 306 I.C.C. 417, 475 (1959), it was stated that the Department of Defense was holding 1,222 sleeping cars on its own storage tracks and planned to acquire 300 more. One wonders where all these sleepers are today.

[9] Milk and cream traffic—along with butterfat and pot cheese—moving at rates quoted per package (as opposed to a weight basis) was for many years regarded as sufficiently distinctive to merit a separate revenue account in the ICC uniform system, *i.e.*, account 109.

For many years, the railroads had sought approval of state regulatory agencies (the ICC had no early jurisdiction) in discontinuing unprofitable passenger trains. However, because of a large number of petitions for such relief having then recently been filed, the committee perceived a need for a comprehensive study of revenue and out-of-pocket expense data applicable to individual long-distance trains still operating, but deemed unprofitable by railroad management. Accordingly, the committee requested such information from the carriers for a sample month, May 1951. This study covered 1,191 noncommuter trains operated by sixty-one railroads. It indicated the loss for that month to have been $7,035,365 or about $84 million when projected to an annual basis.[10]

Following its analysis of the study results, the committee designed a standard format for use by carriers in presenting revenue and cost evidence in train discontinuance applications. Subject to the demands of "public convenience and necessity" and certain state constitutional requirements mandating preservation of residual services, NARUC and its members were amenable in general to permitting discontinuance of trains that could not be made compensatory. However, a few applications were denied on the ground that the railroads had not attempted to make the service reasonably attractive, *e.g.*, one such train was still heated by coal-burning stoves.

Unfortunately, the deficit was not substantially abated by the reductions in train service. Moreover, a change in the ICC's freight/passenger expense separation formula exacerbated the deficit. Specifically in this regard, the federal agency had ordered major reallocations with respect to accounts 249, 404, and 405 (dealing with roadway maintenance and the operation of signals and interlockers, as well as the pay of flagmen engaged in protecting highway crossings).

In March 1956, the ICC instituted on its own motion an investigation of the passenger situation. [A discussion thereof appears in subchapter 9.] NARUC complained that it had had no early knowledge that any such study was being planned, and—upon denial of its request for a prehearing conference—had no advance opportunity to voice its views with respect to such an undertaking. It did, however, participate and introduce evidence at subsequent hearings, held before an ICC examiner. NARUC enunciated its position as favoring preservation of as much of the national passenger system as was feasible.

The committee charged that coal industry witnesses had testified at the hearings in favor of total elimination of passenger service on the ground that it was unprofitable for the railroads, but conveniently remained silent

---

[10] The New York, New Haven and Hartford Railroad reported that its deficit problems were confined to trains operating fewer than fifty miles, *i.e.*, those in commuter service. Thus, contrary to what one might expect, the carrier believed that all of its Boston-New York through trains were profitable.

relative to the inadequacy of rail revenues accruing from the Products of Mines commodity group of which coal is a major segment. (ICC staff studies had shown that revenues derived from such traffic were insufficient to fully reimburse the carriers for the costs they incurred in handling it.)

Moreover, the committee noted that although the ICC investigation was originally instituted to be a fact-finding survey, "Unfortunately, however, the opportunity...proved more than some parties could resist and the Commission permitted the participation in the proceeding of parties totally unconcerned with the public need for passenger train service. These parties turned the investigation into an adversarial proceeding with resultant long delay and inevitable confusion of the record.... [Their] contribution was entirely negative and hindered rather than helped...."

After the examiner made public his proposed report in the investigation proceeding (the principal finding of which was that the most workable solution to the passenger deficit problem was ultimate elimination of the service), the committee forcefully expressed its disappointment: "In keeping with the overall tenor of the proposed report...much of the reference made to [the NARUC evidence] is in a derogatory manner...not calculated to recognize the value of our studies...and does not indicate that the Panel of State Cooperating Commissioners had any part in [its] preparation...."

Further, the committee castigated the examiner for boasting "with ill-concealed glee" of the ICC's then-newly acquired power (codified in Section 13a of the Interstate Commerce Act) to adjudicate passenger train discontinuances.

4. Passenger Deficit Study (John E. Hansbury, 1953)

[This most thought-provoking article by the acting director of the Bureau of Valuation of the Interstate Commerce Commission (ICC) appeared on page 409 in the February 1953 issue of the *I.C.C. Practitioners' Journal*. Many persons in financial and accounting circles of that era would have ventured that, based upon statistical reports filed with the commission or other similar data sources, rail passenger service (including commuter trains) generated annual deficits between one-half and three-quarter billion dollars. However, Mr. Hansbury's analysis purports to show that such figures may have been exaggerated.]

According to the article, application of the ICC formula separating freight and passenger portions of Class I railroads' expense accounts for the year 1950 resulted in a passenger deficit (intercity plus commuter) of about $508 million after deduction of attributable revenues. Such figure consisted of a $334 million excess of operating expenses over operating revenues, $142 million in payroll and property taxes, and $32 million in net rents and joint facilities. However, it is claimed that four downward adjustments should be made to the $508 million deficit figure to reflect the lower total savings actually realizable upon a theoretical elimination of passenger service:

(1) Application of a 15 percent constant expense factor, taken from a special study, to $1.728 billion total passenger operating expenses results in $259.2 million (rounded to $260 million) not actually savable upon elimination, but merely shifted to freight traffic.

(2) Subtraction of the above $260 million from the $334 million passenger operating loss adds $74 million to freight taxable income which, when taxed at a nominal 50 percent rate, results in $37 million additional freight-related income tax.

(3) Application of a 25 percent passenger portion, a figure derived from prior studies, to total U.S. government taxes other than income taxes of $266 million results in $66.5 million (rounded to $66 million) in passenger payroll taxes that could be eliminated. When subtracted from the $142 million total nonincome taxes, $76 million in property taxes remain. Multiplying the latter figure by 40 percent, the portion of eliminated passenger property based upon valuation records, results in $30.4 million (rounded to $30 million) representing taxes on eliminated passenger property. The remaining $46 million constitutes the passenger portion of property taxes common with freight service, all of which would then shift to freight. At a 50 percent income tax rate, $23 million (rounded to $20 million) would be added to the freight service burden.

(4) Application of the 50 percent income tax rate to the rounded $32 million worth of passenger net rents and joint facilities eliminated, causes $16 million to be shifted to freight.

Incorporating the four adjustments ($260 million, $37 million, $20 million, and $16 million) results in an additional $333 million charged to freight upon the theoretical elimination of passenger service. Subtracting this figure from the 1950 formula deficit of $508 million produces an adjusted total deficit of $175 million, equivalent to only 2 percent of that year's freight operating revenues.

As shown above, the operating portion of the 1950 formula deficit was $334 million, but the concomitant increase in the freight operating expenses was $260 million. Therefore, the real operating deficit was the difference between these figures, or only $74 million.

However, if express traffic handled in passenger trains were considered a high-grade freight service, or a 20 percent constant factor (the result obtained in some studies) had been used in the first adjustment above in lieu of the 15 percent, even the $74 million operating deficit shown would be offset. Thus, Mr. Hansbury concluded that the existence of a passenger operating deficit is "very doubtful."

5. Railroad Passenger Service Costs and Financial Results
   (Stanley Berge, 1956)

This is a study by Stanley Berge, professor of transportation, Northwestern University. In addressing the behavior of railroad costs, Professor Berge stated at the outset that one should distinguish between the economic concepts of average cost (total costs divided by the total quantity of output units) and marginal cost (incremental difference between total costs at varying levels of output, divided by such units).

This approach recognized that a large amount of relatively fixed maintenance expenses, interest, and taxes must be added to variable costs, thus establishing a break-even point. Once sufficient revenues were available to recover these costs, the railroad discovered that it had excess line capacity capable of producing additional units of transportation service at marginal cost.

Professor Berge found that during the present century, passenger service had never constituted the principal business of the major carriers; in the immediate past, it generated no more than 15 percent of operating revenues. Similar to situations in agriculture—where a farmer may derive his primary income from growing corn, but augment his earnings by raising livestock on idle pieces of land—railroads engaged primarily in the freight business should seek to utilize their excess capacity for other types of traffic, *e.g.*, passenger.

Moreover, Professor Berge stressed that route utilization was more critical to a railroad than to its competitors (highway, air, water) because, more often than not, it alone acquires and pays taxes on the right-of-way.

Relative to the matter of accounting for expenses incurred in passenger service, Professor Berge researched the freight/passenger expense separation formula specified by the Interstate Commerce Commission (ICC). He observed that soon after its creation in 1887, the agency required the carriers to report separated expenses when filing their mandatory financial statements. This early procedure may be seen today as lacking refinement, insofar as the instructions directed carriers to allocate common expenses (*e.g.*, those not naturally chargeable to one or the other of the two services) simply on the basis of recorded train-miles irrespective of the number of cars per train, etc.

Dissatisfaction with the separation formula, expressed both by railroad management and by state regulatory bodies, led to the ICC's abandoning the procedure in 1894. Nevertheless, still perceiving a need to obtain such data, the agency in 1914 again promulgated a separation of expenses; on this occasion, the rules were generally accepted and became permanent. Beginning in 1936, the ICC required the carriers to report taxes and joint facility and equipment rents on a separated basis.

The separation rules in effect at the time of Professor Berge's study provided for apportionment of track maintenance expense on the basis of relative gross ton-miles of locomotives, cars, and contents (using an average weight per passenger of 150 pounds). Maintenance of buildings and other structures and of rolling equipment reflected the proportions of use. Other expenses and some taxes not directly assignable were apportioned on the basis of all other expenses combined. Federal income taxes mirrored the separation of pretax net railway operating income, excluding nonrail operations and fixed charges.

Professor Berge noted that the separation formula remained controversial, even within the ICC. For example, in addressing the National Industrial Traffic League in November 1954 relative to the previous year's formula deficit of about $700 million, Chairman Richard F. Mitchell observed, "Frankly, I do not agree with our figures. I think we have overstated the deficit to some extent, so I have cut it $200 million and call it a $500 million red figure."

Similarly, some rail industry executives publicly expressed the view that much of the expense charged to passenger service would not be saved if the carriers were to withdraw entirely from the business of transporting persons. In a June 1954 speech before the New York Society of Security Analysts, E.S. Marsh, vice-president, finance, of the Atchison, Topeka and Santa Fe, noted that despite his company's $418,512 in bridge maintenance expense allocated to passenger service the preceding year, "There isn't a bridge that could be done away with if we had no passenger trains."

Professor Berge commented approvingly upon a study of profitable "name trains" performed by Coverdale & Colpitts (C&C), New York consulting engineers. Of the fifteen trains in the study for which Professor Berge reproduced year 1948 data, total revenue per train-mile ranged from a low of $2.32 for the eight-car Nebraska Zephyr to a high of $8.64 for the nineteen-car Morning Daylight. The corresponding net revenue figures for these two trains were $1.29 and $4.65, respectively.[11]

---

[11] The other thirteen trains in the C&C study (listed in ascending order of total revenue per train-mile) were as follows: Des Moines Rocket, Twin Star Rocket, Peoria Rocket, Corn Belt Rocket, Missouri River Eagle, Rocky Mountain Rocket, Colorado Eagle, Twin Zephyrs, Southerner, Tennessean, Capitol Limited, Silver Meteor, Afternoon Hiawatha.

Another publication also reporting on profitable trains—page 96 of *Railway Age* in its May 19, 1952, issue—mentioned the following: Capitol Limited, Blue Bird, California Zephyr, Afternoon Hiawatha, Lark, Nancy Hanks II, George Washington, Kansas City-Florida Special, Humming Bird.

C&C's study so impressed the editors of *Fortune* magazine that a discussion thereof appeared on page 78 in the May 1950 issue. [Another enthusiastic article on rail passenger service was published on page 64 in the March 1964 issue of *Argosy* magazine.]

6. Cost Data for Railroad Passenger Service (Dwight R. Ladd, 1957)

The author of this book, the full title of which is *Cost Data for the Management of Railroad Passenger Service*, was associate professor of business administration at the University of Western Ontario. Previously, he was a professor at Harvard University.

The book begins with an assertion that the railroad industry is characterized by joint operating costs. As an example, Professor Ladd referred to a Boston-to-New York passenger train stopped at the Old Saybrook station. At that point, the train likely was carrying passengers who boarded at origin and were traveling to such intermediate points as New Haven, Bridgeport, or Stamford, as well as to the train's final destination. It also likely had passengers destined to all of those points who boarded at Providence. Earlier in the trip, it may have carried passengers from Westerly to New London. His point was that the cost of providing any one of these movements was unavoidably intertwined with the cost of all the others.

Nevertheless, he believed the fundamental approach which should be taken in analyzing such costs was not inherently different from that pursued in other multiple-product industries. It should be borne in mind, however, that because of divided responsibilities between operating and sales departments, managerial control of railroad costs often may not rest in one location within a company. Also, it may be necessary to involve other companies in instances where an interline service is provided by two or more carriers.

Professor Ladd thought the accounting system prescribed for rail carriers by the Interstate Commerce Commission (ICC) could be successfully adapted for use in managerial cost control. However, in light of the consolidation in account 317 of passenger car maintenance expenses for all car types (ranging from modern coaches having complex air conditioning and lighting to turn-of-the-century wooden baggage cars), it was desirable that carrier management keep subaccounts for each type in order to preserve cost differences.

While encouraging the use of cost centers (where expenses are recorded by function, as in locomotive and car shops), Professor Ladd recognized certain anomalies. For example, the accounting practice followed in recording ticket office transactions differed as to whether a particular ticket was issued at a station or at a downtown sales office.

Professor Ladd noted instances where major coal mine and steel mill strikes caused curtailment of rail freight operations, such that an abnormally large portion of common expenses then shifted to the passenger service. This accounting treatment tended to distort financial statements prepared for the latter.

According to Professor Ladd, innovative management ideas could be stifled through fear that determined regulators may order failed experimental services or fares be kept in perpetuity. Nevertheless, the carriers did possess some flexibility, as evidenced by New York Central's then-recent combining of its Commodore Vanderbilt and Pacemaker trains.

Professor Ladd suggested that expenditures for plant maintenance constitute a greater proportion of total costs for a railroad than for a manufacturer incurring costs of raw material inventories held for processing. However, railroads could sometimes postpone maintenance until periods of relative prosperity, at which time the requisite funds could more easily be made available.

We are reminded that under ICC accounting rules, carriers' expenditures associated with repairing deteriorated track components (rails, ties, ballast, etc.) were charged to expenses in the year of disbursement. Hence, the cost of extensive roadway rehabilitation programs benefited rail traffic for years to come.[12]

Some rail industry executives declared that passenger trains occasion few additional roadway expenses beyond the level required for freight. On the other hand, the then-recent shift east of Omaha of certain Chicago-West Coast trains from the Chicago and North Western to the Milwaukee railroad required an advance expenditure of $2,000,000 for track and signal projects on the latter's line. Indeed, the so-called Yager Formula, then followed by the American Railway Engineering Association, estimated roadway maintenance expenses as one-third variable with changes in traffic. Two large railroads (Southern Pacific and Canadian National), applying standard statistical techniques of time series and cross-sectional analysis, purportedly derived variabilities of almost 60 percent.

Professor Ladd posed the question of whether changes in passenger volume would result in proportionate changes in direct and indirect costs. His answer was that some costs are related to individual trains and others to the service itself, such as the general passenger department office. He observed specifically that upon the Rutland Railroad's discontinuance of all passenger service, that carrier's management claimed to have made its freight operations more efficient by consolidating the locations of previously scattered facilities.

---

[12] While Professor Ladd's assertion was true when made in 1957, the ICC later prescribed depreciation for such track accounts.

Relative to determining operating costs of existing trains, Professor Ladd asserted that while cost analysts may find certain underlying accounting data difficult to ferret out, crew wage payments were usually accessible because of legal requirements to maintain payroll tax records. Additionally, he cautioned against blanket use of systemwide unit costs expressed on a per train-mile basis, an approach which would wrongfully equate fuel consumed by, *e.g.*, a two-car local with that of a sixteen-car express operating the same distance. He further counseled that costs incurred by station switch crews during idle moments between train arrivals and departures should be charged to the trains they switch.

Professor Ladd took note of certain special passenger train movements: U.S. government movements on the Erie Railroad; a series of convention trains to Miami on the Seaboard Air Line; hunters' specials on Canadian National; Bowie (Maryland) Race Track trains on the Pennsylvania Railroad; student specials on Chicago, Burlington and Quincy; and a Yale University football special on the New York, New Haven and Hartford.

The carriers deemed these special trains profitable on the theory that since the tracks were already in place and the cars would otherwise have continued "rusting in the yards," the only costs incurred were incremental in nature. Professor Ladd admonished, however, that special passenger movements could impede freight operations, interfere with track maintenance schedules, and suffer abuse from boisterous sports fans celebrating team victories.

He also discussed the revenue and cost considerations of certain carrier actions. These included consolidating Cleveland-Youngstown trains on the Erie Railroad, adding late evening stops for theatre patrons returning home on New Haven's southbound Quaker, eliminating Illinois Central's last remaining Louisville service, and discontinuing a Southern Pacific midday Oakland Pier-Sacramento roundtrip.

Finally, Professor Ladd commented that the Chesapeake and Ohio Railway had developed a particularly sophisticated approach to ascertaining its passenger service costs.

7. Passenger Train Costs (Aeronautical Research Foundation, 1957)

The Association of American Railroads (AAR) financed this study—the precise title of which is *Avoidable Costs of Passenger Train Service*—in response to a notice issued by the Bureau of Accounts, Cost Finding and Valuation of the Interstate Commerce Commission (ICC). That notice had asked for public comment relative to a passenger train costing methodology then being developed by ICC staff personnel.

Because of conflicting views on the subject prevailing within the railroad industry, AAR arranged for the independent Aeronautical Research Foundation (ARF) to design the study. ARF characterized itself as a nonprofit group dealing primarily with matters of air transportation economics. It saw the matter of rail passenger costs in a regulatory setting as "one of the great modern enigmas."

The ICC was seeking a means for evaluating the passenger service as a whole, as well as individual trains. It tentatively set forth a cost methodology based upon the "least squares" regression formula ($Y = a + bX$) where Y equals the total operating expenses per mile of road or track and X designates the ratio of total gross ton-miles to total road or track mileage, *i.e.*, traffic density. The federal agency considered the results to be determinative of the "percent variable," a factor applied to recorded expenses to obtain estimates of their variable portions.

ARF suggested that the ICC should have augmented its straight ton-mile basis of allocating common and fixed costs with such additional factors as locomotive-miles and yard engine-hours, coupled with a disaggregation of total costs into smaller components for individual treatment. Moreover, ARF asserted that when railroads in the ICC's regressions were plotted with nonrandom stochastic deviations from average or central tendency (*i.e.*, the regression values are either all positive or all negative), consistent over- or underestimates were inevitable. Lastly, ARF claimed the ICC approach implicitly held existing track-miles as a constant, thus ignoring the long-run contraction in plant size that elimination of passenger service might allow.

Having commented upon the ICC methodology, ARF next described its own preferred technique. Accordingly, to derive variable and fixed costs, it adopted multiple-variate cost functions incorporating a statistical cross-section of U.S. railroads. As an example, ARF's formula for projecting certain roadway maintenance accounts reflected the following: (1) threshold costs covering the minimum amount allowing the railroad enterprise, with access to modern technology, to remain a going concern; (2) output costs, measured in gross ton-miles; and (3) size costs, predicated upon miles of track.

These three factors were plotted on a three-dimensional plane (as opposed to a simple two-dimensional graph suitable for depicting the ICC proposal) having the minimum sum of squares of the vertical distances from the plane to the plotted points. All points on the plane collectively represented the total cost corresponding to a selected combination of output and size characteristics. Two derivative slopes on the plane defined the effect upon costs arising from variations in (1) gross ton-miles, with miles of track held constant; and (2) miles of track, with gross ton-miles held constant.

In applying the results of the studies described above, ARF used the following six-step procedure: (1) define the cost categories narrowly enough so that each can be suitably explained by variations in a limited set of output and size variables; (2) examine the nature of the items in such categories in order to identify possible explanatory variables; (3) determine the combination of variables producing the highest R^2 value[13]; (4) calculate raw slope coefficients of retained variables; (5) adjust coefficients for the so-called "pyramid effect," caused by interrelationships between size and quantity variables, and for negative constants; and (6) insert the sum of all investment threshold cost.

ARF adapted its methodology to twenty-seven railroads for the year 1955. The empirical results suggested that "avoidable" costs aggregated about $1,680,000,000. (By contrast, the ICC reported for these carriers "solely related" costs of $1,100,000,000 and "full" costs of $1,478,000,000.) Expanding its cost figure to embrace smaller railroads excluded from the basic study, ARF increased the total to $1,975,000,000. According to ARF, its methodology can be used to cost individual trains.

With total passenger service revenues of $1,267,000,000 for 1955, ARF calculated a deficit of $708,000,000 (or $604,000,000 if ICC-prescribed book asset depreciation had been used in lieu of the cost of reproduction, and $554,000,000 if certain less tangible investment savings had also been omitted).[14]

8. Passengers and Profit (Railway Progress Institute, 1959)

Railway Progress Institute (RPI)—whose members are composed principally of firms engaged in the manufacture of equipment, facilities, and supplies used by railroads—had become aware of the growing passenger train losses being sustained by the carriers in the 1950s. There was general apprehension that if service were curtailed as a result, the market for their products would diminish.

Hence, at RPI's 1956 annual meeting, a resolution was approved which called for taking whatever action was necessary to assure that those trains still well patronized would be enabled to continue operating. The following year, an RPI committee chaired by an executive of the Pullman-Standard Car Manufacturing Company commissioned the independent research firm Transportation Facts, Inc., to undertake a basic economic study of the nation's rail passenger service.[15]

The study first examined some of the developments having occurred earlier in the century that gave rise to the competitive conditions then

---

[13] In a regression, R^2 is the coefficient of determination, *i.e.*, the percent of variation in the dependent variable that is explained by the independent variable(s). The nearer this coefficient comes to 100% (perfect correlation), the better.

[14] The ARF study is discussed at 306 I.C.C. 417, 424-7 (1959). For a brief review, see James C. Nelson, *Railroad Transportation and Public Policy*, The Brookings Institution (1959), pages 300-301. At the time, that author was on leave from the faculty at Washington State University.

facing the railroads. For example, it discussed the rapid growth of automobile use in the 1920s. Addressing regional differences, the study showed that to retain passengers, the southern carriers—operating in an area of lower per capita incomes—had found it necessary to hold down fare levels. The study also illustrated the disparate effects of the Great Depression, whereas while by 1932 first class traffic had declined to a level half that of a decade earlier, two-thirds of the coach passengers had been lost; on the other hand, coach traffic began its postdepression recovery sooner.

During the height of World War II, the immense increase in long distance travel led to passenger traffic generating a quarter of all Class I railroad revenues. After the peak war years, total rail passenger volume again declined. However, western traffic held stable largely through carriers in that territory having met the demand for streamliner service by making theretofore triweekly trains daily. Transcontinental traffic was, however, harmed somewhat through significant fare increases published by eastern connecting lines.

Regarding intermodal comparisons, the study stated that passenger trains incur the lowest operating costs. That is to say, based upon data obtained from the Interstate Commerce Commission and the Civil Aeronautics Administration, 1957-level costs to provide 100 seat-miles were as follows: 60-seat luxury rail coaches-$1.00; 37-seat buses-$1.08; 70-seat DC-6 airplanes-$3.14. Rail's overall poor financial performance was explained by a utilization of capacity at only 30-35 percent, *vis-a-vis* 60 percent for buses and 70 percent for airplanes.

Additionally, the train was seen to possess an advantage its competing modes cannot match, *viz.*, it could split its journey at midpoint and proceed to separate destinations. Moreover, a train usually paused at intermediate stations only for about five minutes, whereas fifteen to thirty were commonly added for an airliner or a bus. Further, overnight trains allowed travelers to avoid hotel expenses.

The authors observed that despite traffic fluctuations over a period of years, the railroads' average operating expense per car-mile (adjusted for constant dollars) consistently fell within the 58- to 61-cent range. Accordingly, they regarded such expense as the break-even point below which average revenue should not be allowed to drop.

For the year 1955, they analyzed the various rail car types separately in an effort to determine how the expense of each related to that year's average of about 61 cents. An allowance was made for $125 million in Pullman Company expenses, less the $30 million of Pullman charges

---

[15] Another author (Donald M. Itzkoff, *Off the Track*, Greenwood Press [1985], page 55) commented on an article discussing this subject that appeared in *Newsweek*, September 12, 1960, pages 79-80. Additionally, excerpted data appeared on pages 274 and 299-302 of a task force report (dated January 3, 1961) prepared for the U.S. Senate Committee on Interstate and Foreign Commerce.

made against the railroads (approximately the difference between Pullman space revenue and Pullman expenses).[16]

According to the study results, after mail and express cars—which had, at 46.6 cents per car-mile, the lowest expense of all car categories because they generated less depreciation and did not bear an advertising expense allocation—intercity coaches incurred the next lowest at 55.8 cents; sleeping and parlor cars incurred 69.3 cents, excluding the Pullman additive; suburban commuter coaches, which ran few miles, incurred 80.6 cents; dining and lounge cars incurred the highest expense at 97.7 cents, including a net of 34.4 cents in food expense and 24.6 cents in food revenue.

The authors used the above expenses for the various car types to hypothesize how a restructuring of the passenger service could lead to elimination of operating deficits. Specifically, the following modifications would be made to conventional practices:

(1) Reduce labor expenses through employment of three-man crews working seven hours daily.

(2) Reduce car expenses through judicious use of 80-seat coaches (without venetian blinds) and 36-berth sleeping cars, each with several "triple decker" rooms.

(3) Reduce maintenance expenses through retirement of older head-end cars and improved utilization of the remainder, resulting in a halving of car-miles operated.

(4) Reduce motive power requirements through reduction in the trailing weight of coaches and head-end cars eliminated in steps 2 and 3.

(5) Reduce running maintenance-of-way expenses through reduction in the trailing weight in step 4.

(6) Reduce servicing requirements through reduction in the number of cars in step 2.

(7) Reduce general expenses on a pro rata, car-mile basis through fewer car-miles operated in steps 2 and 3.

---

[16] As information, leasing arrangements with The Pullman Company terminated on January 1, 1969, for all U.S. railroads.

(8) Reduce equipment depreciation through replacement of dining and lounge cars with "sit-down" space in each car for 16-20 persons served limited-choice menu items warmed by a stewardess.[17]

(9) Eliminate free transportation of company employees and mail.

According to the study, implementation of the above modifications converted the 1955 passenger operating deficit of $447.5 million (after deducting the net loss from commuters) into an intercity net operating income of $301 million. The latter amount would contribute toward nonoperating taxes, rentals, and interest.

9. Railroad Passenger Train Deficit (Interstate Commerce Commission, 1959)

Based upon a statute directing the Interstate Commerce Commission (ICC) to "keep itself informed as to the manner and method in which" railroads conduct their business, the agency instituted an investigation in Docket No. 31954 covering all aspects of passenger train service. Following public hearings held before an examiner, a proposed report was issued. Various parties filed exceptions and replies thereto. The commission's formal report of this investigation appears at 306 I.C.C. 417 (1959). [18]

A study titled *Avoidable Costs of Passenger Train Service*, financed by the Association of American Railroads (AAR) and prepared by the Aeronautical Research Foundation (ARF), was introduced into evidence. [The ARF study was discussed in some detail in subchapter 7.] ARF's methodology purported to show passenger service deficits of greater magnitude than those calculated by the ICC. Commenting, the U.S. General Services Administration claimed the use therein of multiple regression or correlation, while possibly proving fruitful at some future time, had been applied in a "demonstrably erroneous" manner such that the resulting cost estimates "are far too unreliable to be accorded any practical significance."

Contrastingly, the National Coal Association believed the ARF study to be "a landmark in statistical costing...that...provides the best answer to date to the thorny question of the size of the passenger deficit...[and] that the statistical methods used are superior to those used in other studies of

---

[17] As support for the feasibility of eliminating dining cars, the study referred to a modest number of Pullman Company-operated, combination sleeping-lounge cars offering light meals and beverages served by the car attendant. Pullman reported the operation as profitable. In the late 1960s, this author had occasion to use such service on Union Pacific's Butte Special. In both directions, that train departed from its origins after the beginning of what is generally regarded as normal dinner hours and arrived at the destinations very early the next morning. Consequently, the demand for meals was limited. Whether the attendant could have satisfactorily served for a complete dinner or breakfast period, while continuing to perform his other duties, is a question for consideration.

the problem." The railroads expressed no opinion as to the practical value of the ARF study for the future, despite the AAR having funded it.

The ICC was disinclined to incorporate any multiple regression or correlation technique into its existing freight/passenger cost separation formula, stating that the current rules satisfied its needs for rate determination. Moreover, the agency questioned the coal association's belief that adopting such an approach would be "relatively simple, quick and inexpensive." Additionally, it found that further analysis separating the overall deficit among the various kinds of service offered (*i.e.*, coach, parlor, dining, sleeping, and head-end traffic) would unwisely prolong the investigation.

The report also noted that the passenger service was undergoing a cost-revenue squeeze, characterized by rising wage rates and material prices on one hand and a declining traffic base lost to highway and air competition on the other. Significantly, the average hourly compensation of railroad employees, a critical measure in such a labor-intensive industry, had increased 74 percent in the preceding ten years.

Regarding revenue, the ICC observed that the principal eastern railroads maintained first class fares, including Pullman Company charges, at a level generally higher than air fares. It did note, however, that coach sleepers (slumbercoaches) then operating on one eastern and one western line were enjoying 92 percent occupancy, with 80 percent the break-even point.

Most of the new, experimental equipment then being tested (Talgo, Train X, Xplorer) was not deemed widely successful because coupler incompatibility precluded attaching conventional cars during peak travel periods. Nevertheless, in view of the carriers having increased their locomotive and car fleet investment by about a half-billion dollars since the end of World War II, the ICC believed they could not fairly be charged with undue conservatism. Moreover, from the year 1936 (when the statistic first was published) to 1957 (the latest year for which figures were available), average passenger train speed had increased 18 percent.

There was a discussion relative to labor union agreements tending to unduly boost wage expenses of passenger train crews. For example, a Great Northern fireman on the 109-mile, Minot-New Rockford run in North Dakota pocketed more than a full day's pay for operating just two hours and eleven minutes. Eight engine crews, collectively receiving a total of 10 1/3 basic days' pay, were required on the Burlington's 1,034-mile, 16 1/2-hour Denver Zephyr run. The Railway Labor Executives'

---

[18] The lay press sometimes referred to the outcome of the investigation as the "Hosmer Report," after Howard Hosmer, the assigned ICC examiner. This examiner's proposed report included an oft-quoted speculative conclusion that railway passenger coaches would likely soon become museum pieces along with stagecoaches, sidewheelers, and steam locomotives. Such language was not adopted in the subsequent formal ICC decision.

Association (intervening on behalf of the unionized employees) claimed, however, that if there were "featherbedding" in the rail industry, it could be found in management, where the number of managers allegedly had remained almost constant since 1923, while rank-and-file employment had declined to less than half the number employed in that earlier year.

As to mail and express handled in passenger service, the ICC stated that although revenue accruing from the former had increased from World War II levels, prospects for the latter were "clouded with uncertainty."

Relative to concerns of inequitable tax treatment, the ICC noted that New York Central (NYC) had paid a property tax of $59,904 on its Albany, New York, station in 1956, a year in which that city's municipally-owed airport incurred a $57,784 deficit. In 1950, NYC was pressured to spend $4,856,745 on a new passenger station in Toledo, Ohio, while an airport financed with public funds a few years later incurred a 1957 deficit of $16,366. Great Northern was assessed 1956 airport levies of $2,241 at Cut Bank, Montana, while Western Airlines paid an *ad valorem* tax of only $22.92. Cook County, Illinois, collected $12,018,985 in 1985 property taxes on rail passenger stations and only $238,360 from the twelve major airlines having facilities there. In 1956, New Jersey—assessing property taxes at 100 percent of value, compared with a lower basis for other taxpayers—levied taxes against the railroads at more than five times the national average per mile of road.

The ICC concluded its report on the passenger deficit with an overview of the situation then prevailing. This author believes the following passages are of such import as to warrant direct quoting:

> This proceeding and congressional hearings in 1958 relating to railroad problems, as well as other factors, have attracted much public attention to the declining fortunes of railroad passenger service. There has been considerable and perhaps undue emphasis on statistical trends interpreted as a portent of the eventual disappearance of that service within 10 or 12 years, if railroad passenger-miles continue to decline at the average rate of reduction between 1947 and 1957. Whether those trends are indeed so ominous as to signify the eventual demise of railroad passenger service is a matter of opinion. One thing, however, is abundantly clear. For more than a quarter of a century, excepting the brief span of World War II, the expense of performing this service has regularly exceeded associated revenues. The financial loss is real; it is large and appears to be growing; and it endangers the present and future welfare of the railroad industry.

* * * * *

Figures for 1958 show that for the first time in the 70 years of recorded history of the American railroads, their passengers numbered less than 400 million. This decline has occurred against a background of an expanding population with more time, means, and the desire for travel....

*****

In view of the changed demand occasioned by the growing preference for service provided by other forms of transportation, it appears that railroad management should develop, on an industrywide basis, policies and plans for reconstituting railroad passenger service into a less extensive network more closely tailored to the needs of the public....

10. Rail Passenger Traffic in the West (Stanford Research Institute, 1966)

This piece by Stanford Research Institute (SRI), the full title of which is *The Future of Rail Passenger Traffic in the West*, was commissioned by the Southern Pacific Company (SP) to examine the causes of a post-World War II decline in rail passenger traffic and to hypothesize the future of the service. It embraced all western railroads operating passenger trains, but focused upon four long-distance routes in which SP was either the sole operator or a significant participant, *viz.*, San Francisco-Los Angeles, San Francisco-Chicago, Los Angeles-Chicago, and Los Angeles-New Orleans.

SRI proceeded to inform us that private automobiles had become the travel mode for the masses. It maintained that automobile owners, having likely acquired their vehicles with short-distance utility in mind, saw the cost of long trips as nothing more than incremental outlays. Moreover, SRI was impressed by the "combination of powerful engines and improved highways." It further averred that automobile drivers could select their time of departure at whim and forsake use of taxicabs, etc., for local travel at destination.

Furthermore, some older-generation rail patrons were believed to select train travel because they acquired a predilection therefor early in life when there were fewer alternatives. Conversely, younger persons might not become loyal passenger train customers because they had grown up accustomed to having a choice of modes. Possible development of a new generation of equipment possessing the capability of reviving public interest in western rail travel was not expected in the near term because the nation's technical resources required to accomplish such a task were then fully deployed in reengineering the Pennsylvania Railroad's Northeast Corridor line.

SRI also claimed that businessmen craved air service which enabled them to span "vast distances...with little loss in work time." Support for this contention was allegedly found in (1) a 1963 survey by the Bureau of the Census asserting that fifteen businessmen traveled by air for every two traveling by rail;[19] and (2) the record in a discontinuance hearing involving SP's overnight San Francisco-Los Angeles express train known as the Lark, wherein an official of a large company [not identified by SRI] testified that of its staff personnel collectively making 3,000 annual trips between the two cities, those choosing rail over air purportedly constituted something less than 3 percent.[20]

There was presented a comparison of costs incurred by the several transportation modes to provide service in this San Francisco-Los Angeles market. Thus, SRI made a study purporting to reveal per passenger "direct" costs for rail of $18.41 (derived from SP records covering operation of its Coast Daylight, but excluding maintenance-of-way expenses) and for air of $9.89 (reflecting Boeing 727 data obtained from the Civil Aeronautics Board). SRI also showed a direct cost for bus of $9.11 (furnished by Greyhound).[21]

Finally, SRI acknowledged that the "hard pursuit" of a passenger deficit-reduction policy, practiced by some railroads, had aroused considerable public opposition. The consequence had been the emergence of very vocal protesters, resulting in a tainting of the carriers' public images.[22]

Such a policy, which had undoubtedly influenced regulatory commissions in their deliberations, was seen as partially self-defeating. Thus, in discontinuance proceedings adjudicated by the Interstate Commerce

---

[19] For reasons known only to itself, SRI failed to tell us how many of the fifteen businessmen traveled between places for which rail service was not an option. The true basis for their selection of air as the mode of travel cannot be determined without this statistic.

[20] An article on profitable passenger trains in *Railway Age* of May 19, 1952, disclosed on page 99 that the Lark then carried eleven sleeping cars. (Overnight coach passengers were handled on the Coaster, operating in advance of the Lark.) Based upon *The Official Register of Passenger Equipment* (The Railway Equipment and Publication Co., New York, 1961), SP's sleepers had berth capacities ranging from 23 to 27 persons. Using 25 as a simple average, the Lark would have had 275 total berths. Its reported revenue/out-of-pocket-cost ratio of 124 percent suggests that the 1952 break-even point might have been about 222 passengers.

SRI did not provide us with the Lark's capacity or load factor at the time of the discontinuance hearing, although presumably by the 1960s the train's patronage had declined. It is interesting to note, however, that the diversion of only a small portion of airborne travelers would have enabled it to regain the traffic lost.

Using SRI's figures as input for the following calculations, in 1965 there were 763 weekly San Francisco-Los Angeles air flights. Based upon an average of 83 passengers per flight, there would have been 9,047 total daily passengers, or 4,524 in each direction. Considering that 56 percent of all air passengers traveled on business (the Lark's traditional market), 2,533 such persons were potential rail patrons. This number constituted the equivalent of 9.2 sold-out, 11-sleeping car trains. With such a huge volume of persons traveling, it would seem that a little advertising could have helped fill unsold space.

However, in the period 1950-1965, SP reduced its passenger advertising by 90 percent. This came as another large western carrier (Northern Pacific Railway or NP) doubled its advertising and saw its passenger-miles climb from 275 million in 1950 to a 1955 peak of 346 million. After a brief decline to 323 million in 1960, the figure started rising again, reaching 332 million by 1965 (the last year of SRI data). In that final five-year period, NP's passenger-miles increased by 2.7 percent, while its deficit rose only 2.4 percent. Thus, it is difficult for critics to argue that the continued increase in passenger traffic was unduly aggravating the deficit.

Commission, the number of railroad petitions denied or dismissed (expressed as a percentage of petitions granted) increased from 28 percent in fiscal year 1964 to 32 percent in fiscal 1965 and 37 percent in fiscal 1966.

11. Intercity Rail Passenger Service (Interstate Commerce Commission, 1968)

In June 1968, ten years after Congress conferred upon the Interstate Commerce Commission (ICC) final administrative authority over discontinuance of rail passenger service through the new Section 13a of the Interstate Commerce Act, that agency submitted this report jointly to the Senate Committee on Commerce and the House Interstate and Foreign Commerce Committee. The purpose of the report was to inform Congress of developments concerning its execution of the new powers it had acquired under the legislation.

The ICC observed that after enactment of Section 13a, the rate of passenger train discontinuances accelerated sharply. For example, during the decade 1958-67, the number of trains performing intercity service (*i.e.*, those having runs exceeding seventy-five miles) dropped from 1,448 to 590, a decline of 59.3 percent. The miles of road over which such trains were operated declined from 104,964 to 67,035 or by 36.1 percent. Thirteen Class I railroads ceased all regular passenger service. Moreover, for the remaining business, the carriers had slackened in their promotional efforts and in their willingness to invest further capital.

---

[21] SRI revealed that its calculated rail cost per passenger of $18.41 for the San Francisco-Los Angeles run was derived by dividing total train costs by an average of 170 through passengers (*i.e.*, passengers handled over the entire route), notwithstanding an admission that the Coast Daylight actually carried an average of 236 passengers. The difference between these two figures was the count of short-haul patrons.

In this connection, it is critical to note that SP handled Oakland-Los Angeles passengers in cars coupled to San Francisco-Los Angeles trains at San Jose. South of such point, the cars from both of these origins operated in a consolidated train for 423 miles, or 90 percent of the 470-mile San Francisco-Los Angeles run. (Similarly, northbound passengers from Los Angeles were consolidated into a single train as far as San Jose.) Because it was more efficient for a railroad to consolidate passengers into one train for such a long movement, the railroad's cost per passenger was considerably less than if separate trains were run.

Therefore, SRI should either have deducted the costs attributed to the Oakland cars south of San Jose from the total San Francisco-Los Angeles train costs, or alternatively, offset such costs with the San Jose-Los Angeles portion of the revenue received from Oakland passengers (which is most of it). SRI did neither.

Also, SRI's modal comparison was misleading for its failure to recognize the air transport facility costs borne by government.

[22] Some railroads (but apparently not SP) recognized the goodwill derivable from offering a respectable passenger service. For example, residents of track-side communities annoyed by train noise and motor vehicle drivers blocked at grade crossings by slow-moving freight trains were believed more likely to be tolerant if the rail carrier had built and nurtured a good neighbor image. A corollary benefit was that local city councilmen were probably not quite so eager to enact penalizing ordinances harmful to the railroad's freight business if their constituents were well served by the passenger department.

In that same 10-year period, there had been a reported 39.5 percent decline in the number of intercity revenue passengers. (The ICC deemed the accuracy of this figure suspect, however, because some persons previously purchasing single tickets for use on commuter trains—as opposed to multiple-ride tickets—may have erroneously appeared in the earlier records as intercity passengers.) Measured by passenger-miles, coach traffic had declined by 41.0 percent and parlor and sleeping car traffic by 69.3 percent. Total intercity passenger revenues had fallen 44.9 percent.

While the deficit (defined here as reflecting the total of solely passenger-related expenses and the passenger portion of common expenses) had declined from $723.6 million in 1957 to $408.0 million in 1967, there were indications that it would soon begin rising again. That is to say, actions by the Post Office Department in eliminating railway post office cars, equipped for en route mail sorting, had caused a number of passenger trains to be transformed from marginal to heavy-deficit operations.[23]

In its report to Congress, the ICC noted that since the inception of Section 13a, it had received 267 interstate discontinuance cases and 51 intrastate cases. Based on cases decided before June 1, 1968, the railroads had discontinued 913 trains in whole or in part. About 80 percent of these cases involved intercity trains. Additional trains were discontinued through state proceedings.

The ICC made certain recommendations to Congress in an effort to protect passengers' interests. For example, whereas the statute did not mandate that both of the railroads participating in a two-line movement post advance notice to the public when only one of them wished to discontinue its portion, the ICC believed each should be compelled to do so. Additionally, the agency considered it desirable to legislate special considerations for the last train on a route.

Moreover, the ICC perceived abuse in certain railroads' practice of discontinuing an interstate train in stages. Thus, for each of the various states through which a particular train passed, authority was sought from the state regulatory commission to discontinue the intrastate portion between the station closest to the border of one adjacent state and the station closest to the border of the opposite adjacent state. Assuming that each involved state granted the intrastate discontinuance authority sought, nothing then remained of the former interstate train except a series of short runs crossing the various state borders for which hardly any

---

[23] The loss of RPO cars was a major phenomenon in those days. This author is in possession of a letter from the assistant special assistant to the Postmaster General dated October 10, 1967. It transmitted a list of 127 trains, operating on twenty-one railroads, scheduled to lose their RPO cars in the period September 16-October 28, 1967. Missouri Pacific, exclusive of its Texas and Pacific subsidiary, accounted for sixteen such trains, the most of any railroad.

protestant could prove public need. Accordingly, the railroad then had no difficulty—in another round of hearings, this time before the ICC—demonstrating that discontinuance of these pitiful remnants of the former through train was justified.

The ICC's Section 13a power was soon challenged. Relative to two Southern Railway trains operating between Greensboro and Goldsboro, North Carolina (with a through New York sleeper handled northbound on the Crescent and southbound on the Peach Queen), the state commission had issued an order denying a carrier application for discontinuance. That order was upheld by the state supreme court. 254 N.C. 73, 118 S.E.2d 21 (1961). Thereafter, ruling on a Section 13a petition, the ICC permitted discontinuance. A U.S. District Court, however, set aside the ICC order on the ground that the carrier's offsetting profits from freight operations had not been properly considered, and hence, the decision was arbitrary and capricious. 210 F.Supp. 675 (1962).

Upon appeal to the United States Supreme Court, probable jurisdiction was noted. 373 U.S. 907 (1963). Following argument, the court held that in applying Section 13a, the ICC needed to consider only the effect which discontinuance of a particular train would have upon public convenience and necessity and upon interstate commerce. Holding that the ICC had adhered to the governing standard, the high court reversed the District Court and remanded the case, with instructions to reinstate the ICC order allowing discontinuance. *Southern Railway v. North Carolina*, 376 U.S. 93, 105 (1964).

That the commission did not grant all Section 13a petitions brought to it was shown by the following language used in denying a petition for discontinuing a pair of trains once known as the Imperial:

> The evidence in this proceeding makes it abundantly clear that Southern Pacific has continued to discourage use of these trains by passengers. In fact, it has intensified its efforts in that direction. Whenever it appears, as it does in this proceeding, that a carrier has deliberately downgraded its service in order to justify discontinuance of a train irrespective of the actual or potential needs of the traveling public, the Commission will order the service to be continued. *** The Commission will not find burdens on interstate commerce within the meaning of section 13a of the act to be "undue" if those burdens are voluntarily created by carriers for the purpose of obtaining a favorable decision from the Commission. *Southern Pacific Co. Discontinuance of Train Nos. 39 and 40 Between Tucumcari, New Mexico, and Phoenix, Arizona*, 328 I.C.C. 360, 365 (1966).

Five months later, the ICC approved the report and recommended order of its hearing examiner in Finance Docket No. 23756, which required continuance of Southern Pacific's Shasta Daylight (operating between

Oakland, California and Portland, Oregon) after protestants had shown with "unmistakable clarity that the carrier had discouraged passenger traffic."

In another proceeding, the ICC held that Burlington Northern Inc. (successor to the Northern Pacific Railway, one of several railroads merged into it) was bound by promises "carefully stated under oath" to retain both the Mainstreeter and the North Coast Limited if the merger application were approved. According to the evidence presented, these trains were "heavily patronized" and the "number of passengers has been increasing...." *Northern Pacific Railway Discontinuance—Fargo to Seattle-Tacoma*, 333 I.C.C. 15, 39 (1968).

The ICC noted it had submitted recommendations to the executive branch to improve intercity service generally, including a proposal that it join with the Department of Transportation in conducting a study leading toward identification of "an essential national rail passenger system." The agency believed that "The wholesale collapse of all noncorridor intercity service is not imminent, but the prognosis is grave—fatal in some areas." Lastly, it stated that "The absence of positive policy and actual involvement at the Federal level...cannot help but reinforce the present downward trend.

12. Investigation of Costs of Intercity Rail Passenger Service
    (Interstate Commerce Commission, 1969)

In a letter dated October 8, 1968, to Chairman Paul J. Tierney of the Interstate Commerce Commission (ICC), Senator Warren G. Magnuson, chairman of the Senate Committee on Commerce, requested an investigation of "the actual net costs to the railroads in providing intercity rail passenger service and the means for reducing or meeting such costs." A similar letter dated October 15, 1968, from Congressman Harley O. Staggers, chairman of the House Interstate and Foreign Commerce Committee, stated that such an investigation "could ultimately lay to rest the issue of how much the railroads actually lose...."

Accordingly, after consulting with various entities,[24] the ICC established an *ad hoc* staff committee to oversee a study. Assisting was Wyer, Dick & Co., an independent consulting firm.

To assure completion in time for consideration during the first session of the 91st Congress, the study was confined to the intercity passenger service of eight large- or medium-size carriers operating in all areas of the country except the Northeast, where it was feared extensive commuter

---

[24] Federal Railroad Administration, Association of American Railroads, Railway Labor Executives' Association, National Association of Regulatory Commissioners, National Association of Railroad Passengers.

operations would distort the results.[25] Collectively, these eight railroad systems accounted for 59.5 percent of the 1968 nationwide solely related deficit and 44.1 percent of the full deficit.

The first step in the study was directing the eight carriers to determine for the year 1968 the expenses (labor, materials, etc.) they would not have incurred if there had been no intercity passenger service. Additionally, the ICC asked these carriers to project the alternative cost of moving company personnel and mail then handled in passenger trains. To supplement the foregoing expenses, they were requested to provide inventories of road and equipment property used in their passenger operations, and to identify the probable disposition of such assets.

To obtain a high degree of uniformity, the ICC proposed guidelines and designed reporting forms. Agency field personnel monitored the data-gathering process.

The ICC discovered systemic errors in several of the eight carriers' 1968 books of account that had resulted in incorrect assignment to passenger service of more than $5.7 million in expenses. It also adjusted downward certain personal injury expenses quantified in 1968 (and hence charged to that year's accounts), but reflecting accidents having occurred in a prior year. Similar downward adjustments were made to eliminate repair and depreciation expenses of mail cars originally built for use in passenger service but then handled exclusively in freight trains. One carrier's reported avoidable fuel expense was revised downward because of its questionable assumption that slow-moving locomotives operating in yard switching service consumed fuel at the same rate consonant for high-speed main lines.

Because of the "unit method" of taxation prevalent in most states, by which going concern value greatly outweighs depreciated property investment as a primary tax determinant, property taxes were usually treated as unavoidable.

The ICC generally accepted the carriers' estimates of mail and express revenues retainable through a diversion of the traffic to freight service. As an example, Great Northern's projection for keeping some such traffic then moving on its Western Star was considered reasonable. Revenues accruing from passengers handled in so-called mixed trains, and credited in the accounts to freight service, were added to passenger revenues.

For the eight carriers, ICC's study found 1968 net avoidable expenses (*i.e.*, the excess of avoidable expenses over nonretainable revenues) of $118.1 million. This figure compares with their solely related and full deficits of $117.8 million and $214.3 million, respectively. The agency stated that these relationships varied among the eight carriers and would

---

[25] Atchison, Topeka and Santa Fe; Chesapeake and Ohio-Baltimore and Ohio; Great Northern; Illinois Central; Missouri Pacific; Seaboard Coast Line; Southern Railway System; Union Pacific.

not necessarily be comparable to the experience of other passenger-carrying railroads. Moreover, due to various employee protection agreements, the carriers would not be able to achieve full cash savings immediately.

Increased profitability arising from elimination of passenger deficits would, of course, result in an increase in the portion of account 532 reflecting federal income taxes. The amount of such taxes was influenced by varying asset service lives and investment credit carryovers or carrybacks, all of which were subject to Internal Revenue Service regulations and determined to lie beyond the scope of the ICC study.

The ICC estimated the salvage value of scrapped material at $25-$30 per ton. Further, an allowance was made for the value of equipment convertible to work train or other productive service. A return on net salvable capital was added to the net avoidable expenses. Based upon recent estimates of actual returns earned on depreciated railroad property investment ranging from 6.0 to 9.5 percent, the total return for the study carriers measured between $4.2 million and $6.6 million.

Because a substantial number of usable cars freed up from the massive early- and mid-1960s service discontinuances were available for the remaining trains, the railroads had suspended normal replacement purchases. The ICC forecast that to sustain passenger operations at the 1968 level, the study carriers would need to resume new car acquisition at a level sufficient to replace 40 percent of their 1,965-car fleet within ten years at a cost in then-current prices of $132 million. Any further discontinuances implemented during that period would, of course, have the effect of reducing the total number of new cars required.

Chapter II
The Amtrak Era: Transition and Postimplementation Studies

The final two subchapters of Chapter I—both of them products of the Interstate Commerce Commission—revealed hints of what might be in the offing, *viz.*, government assumption of the nation's rail passenger network. Indeed, Congress enacted, and President Richard M. Nixon signed, the Rail Passenger Service Act of 1970. This statute created the National Railroad Passenger Corporation, known as Railpax during the early planning period before the Amtrak designation was conceived. The process of revamping the traditional network structure had begun.

1. Basic National Rail Passenger System
   (U.S. Department of Transportation, 1971)

Pursuant to legislative mandate, Secretary of Transportation John A. Volpe prepared a preliminary report containing recommendations on routes to comprise a "Basic System." The report was submitted to Congress, the Interstate Commerce Commission (ICC), state regulatory commissions, local governments, rail carriers, labor organizations, and the public. After these entities provided comment, the secretary issued a final report dated January 28, 1971.

The enabling statute directed the secretary to designate mandatory points between which passenger train service "shall" be provided. To help identify such points, the secretary formulated the following considerations, with no single element overriding:

(1) Availability of alternate transportation modes.

(2) Anticipated rail ridership.

(3) Competitive operating costs *vis-a-vis* other modes.

(4) Integration of services into a national network.

(5) Population of mandatory points served to exceed one million.

(6) No undue burden to the system from serving particular routes.

(7) Flexibility for rapid expansion when economically feasible.

(8) Minimum of capital improvements required.

In applying the foregoing considerations, all long-haul trains then operating were examined. A determination was made as to whether the demand for each such train "warranted its continuance," and if so, whether it "contributed to the connection of the different regions of the country by means of a reasonably direct route." General service characteristics applicable to trains selected for inclusion in the system were as follows:

(1) Schedules set to serve markets at reasonable hours, with running times consistent with requirements of station stops, track conditions, and safety.

(2) Frequency of trains determined by level of patronage.

(3) Connections at major points maintained for maximum promotion of a unified system.

(4) Modern equipment furnished to the extent practicable.

(5) Through cars handled between mandatory points and also elsewhere if market demand and operating conditions allow.

(6) Private-room sleeping cars offered on all overnight journeys of at least six hours during the period midnight-8:00 A.M.

(7) Food service, ranging from snacks to complete meal service, made available on all schedules operating 7:00 A.M.-8:00 P.M. and exceeding two hours trip time.

(8) Lounge space provided on all schedules over six hours.

(9) Parlor car or other first class accommodations assigned where justifiable.

The process described above resulted in the final designation of specific pairs of points between which intercity passenger service was to be run.[26] Although the secretary also identified (as required by statute) multiple routes over which the service "may" be operated, determination of the actual routes and operating rail carriers was left to Amtrak's discretion.

The ICC's role in the route selection process should not be undervalued. In reviewing the meager service designated in the preliminary report, Chairman George M. Stafford characterized the secretary's initial proposed network as "merely a few trunklines with occasional flair-outs...." Indeed, the only service initially proposed for the entire Mountain and Pacific time zones consisted of lines connecting Chicago with Seattle, San Francisco, and Los Angeles.

Consequently, the ICC recommended six "essential" additions (seven if St. Petersburg is counted from both New York and Chicago) and nine "secondary" additions. Of these fifteen, eleven were incorporated into Amtrak's original network; the Laredo service was adopted later.[27]

An appendix to the secretary's final report contained a list of the actions taken on comments received from the various parties. The list identified both (1) the addition of specific train services earlier omitted from the preliminary report; and (2) the recommended services that were rejected in the final report, together with the reasons therefor. All of the rejected recommendations were classified according to one or more of seven reasons:

(1) Inadequate existing and potential ridership.

(2) One or both terminal cities not major population centers.

(3) Rail transportation uncompetitive with other modes.

(4) Track and other facilities of insufficient quality.

(5) Substantial losses suggested by revenue and cost estimates.

(6) Designation of specific routes not mandated.

(7) Authority lacking to require service outside the U.S.

---

26 Boston-New York; New York-Washington, Buffalo, Chicago, Kansas City via St. Louis*, Miami, St. Petersburg*, New Orleans; Washington-Chicago*, St. Louis; Norfolk/Newport News*-Charlottesville-Cincinnati; Detroit-Chicago; Chicago-St. Louis, Cincinnati, Miami, St. Petersburg*, New Orleans, Houston, Seattle, Oakland, Los Angeles; New Orleans-Los Angeles*; Seattle-San Diego*.

* These routes, or a portion thereof, were added after preparation of the preliminary report; all such additions had been recommended by the ICC.

So that readers may have an insight into the secretary's procedure, there are listed in Table 1 three sample routes operated by the privately owned railroads in April 1971 (the final pre-Amtrak month) that were omitted from the Basic System, along with the reasons therefor, using the above numbers.

Table 1
Sample Applications of Route Criteria

(1) Chicago-Portland via Boise	1, 5
(2) Boston-Albany	1, 2, 3, 5
(3) Detroit-Cincinnati	1, 3, 5

There was no description in the report of any analytical process that may have been used by the secretary in determining that these specific numbered reasons were applicable to these particular routes.[28]

[On March 22, 1971, David W. Kendall, chairman of Amtrak's board of incorporators, publicly identified the operational routes for the start-up day, May 1, 1971. Except for Penn Central's Susquehanna River line, used to connect the Baltimore and Harrisburg stations, all routes adopted were a continuation of the private carriers' service.]

2. Reports on Amtrak to the President and Congress
(Interstate Commerce Commission, 1971 ff.)

[The Interstate Commerce Commission (ICC) submitted to Congress a series of reports covering both the transition from private ownership and the early years of Amtrak operation. This subchapter synopsizes the reports and gives an insight into some of the concerns faced in those days.]

Initially, twenty railroads paid their respective fees entitling them to join the Amtrak system. Four of them (Penn Central; Burlington Northern; Chicago, Milwaukee, St. Paul and Pacific; and Grand Trunk Western)

---

[27] ICC Recommendations

Essential	Secondary
1. Seattle-San Diego*	1. Salt Lake City-Butte
2. New Orleans-Los Angeles*	2. St. Louis-Kansas City*
3. Feather River Canyon	3. St. Louis-Detroit
4. Washington-Chicago*	4. Charlottesville-Newport News*
5. St. Paul and Minneapolis*	5. Chicago-Albany-Boston*
6. Tampa and St. Petersburg*	6. Seattle-Vancouver*
	7. Chicago-Toronto*
	8. New York-Montreal*
	9. Chicago-San Antonio-Laredo

* ICC recommendations that were implemented in DOT secretary's report.

[28] Reaching an opposite conclusion in its July 1975 Final System Plan (Volume I at page 43), the United States Railway Association recommended Detroit-Cincinnati as a line "where upgrading for passenger service might return substantial benefits."

became holders of common stock in the corporation. All except the latter held seats on the board; other board members, government and nongovernment, represented the public. There was also appointed a financial advisory panel consisting of members of the investment community who were to receive no compensation.

Railroads desiring to continue operating their own passenger trains were allowed to do so; thus, five chose not to join Amtrak. The Denver and Rio Grande Western claimed that sidetracking of its freight trains by Amtrak would jeopardize its competitive position. The Chicago, Rock Island and Pacific concluded that since its then-current intercity losses roughly equaled the cost of joining, by retaining its trains it would "thereby perform a service to the people of Illinois." Southern Railway and Georgia Railroad also believed that joining would not be beneficial. The fifth, Canadian Pacific, did not furnish information on its reason.

Although Amtrak was exempted from filing tariffs, it remained subject to other regulatory provisions. Noting the passenger carrier exhibited an "initial reluctance to provide access to all of its records," the ICC subsequently came to believe, however, that "smooth lines of communication" had been established and that the attendant problems were "hopefully...resolved."

According to the ICC, insufficient funding for Amtrak was "glaringly evident from the beginning." The entire allotted $40 million federal appropriation was drawn down during the period February 2-August 16, 1971. The private railroads' buy-in fees of $197 million were expected to be fully paid and cease by mid-1974. Amtrak was allowed to receive some equipment from the participating railroads in lieu of cash; accordingly, it acquired 1,200 cars in this manner. Although there was no penalty provision for late payment, Penn Central (PC) soon forfeited $16,565 in interest for its lateness.

Amtrak was obligated to advance to its participating carriers by the fifteenth of each month sufficient monies to defray their anticipated operating deficits. The ICC characterized the financial situation as particularly acute in the mid-1970s, a time of "one of the worst inflationary spirals in recent history."

Because of delay in hiring a permanent staff, Amtrak retained a number of private firms to provide initial technical help. These firms (including one air carrier) worked in the fields of personnel, accounting, engineering, advertising, public relations, real estate, and legal services.

The ICC reported that it saw no indication of Amtrak's planning to establish a meaningful internal audit program. Account postings in the first six months ran significantly behind.

Early on, the public liberally exercised its right to complain to the ICC relative to all kinds of Amtrak service deficiencies. As a result, forty-five of the agency's field personnel conducted 129 investigations in August and September 1971, dealing with such matters as lateness, inadequate sleeping car capacity, air conditioning failures, broken windows, reservation and information shortcomings, etc. Complaints of fare anomalies, arising from Amtrak's amalgamation of multiple tariffs, were difficult to ameliorate because of the then-prevailing "wage-price freeze."

A thirty-seven-page appendix to the ICC's October 1971 report dealt solely with problems arising from scheduling. Here are some examples: Because of less-than-daily operation, a connection was missed from the southbound Cascade Coast to the California Zephyr at Oakland [there being no stops then at the present Martinez junction]; inconvenient connections prevailed at Newton, Kansas, arising from lack of through cars between the Texas Chief and Super Chief; westbound, the James Whitcomb Riley missed the Empire Builder at Chicago; the City of New Orleans and the South Wind missed all inbound and outbound trains at Chicago, and the latter at Indianapolis and Birmingham as well. A theoretical rescheduling, shown in considerable detail, purportedly would have solved some of these problems.

Although there had been a statutory freeze on passenger train discontinuances during the transition period, new procedural duties were placed upon the ICC in connection with Amtrak's start-up. For example, because commuter service was not covered by the legislation, it was necessary for the agency to investigate the status of certain borderline runs to determine if they were subject thereto. Thus, it found that although PC trains between New York City and Chatham, New York, operated a relatively short distance, they were nevertheless intercity in nature. Later, the ICC adjudicated disputes with the Texas and Pacific and Central Vermont railways relative to facilitating operation of the Inter-American and Montréaler, respectively.

Also, the ICC instituted a proceeding (*Ex Parte* No. 268) to establish a formula for calculating the amount of "avoidable losses" for use in establishing the fees that the carriers would pay to join Amtrak. Another proceeding (*Ex Parte* No. 339) concerned through routes and joint fares with motor passenger carriers and coordination with the other rail carriers, the principal example of the latter being the handling of Auto Train Corporation cars on Amtrak's Floridian between Louisville, Kentucky, and Sanford, Florida.

By 1976, Amtrak's new equipment acquisitions allowed nearly half its passengers to ride in cars less than three years of age.

As part of the ICC's monitoring process, agency staff personnel inspected 490 stations. Some of these visits were unannounced. Since much of the surveillance occurred during peak holiday periods, these inspectors exercised the opportunity to extend personal assistance to many travelers.

The inspection program also took place on moving trains. Although the ICC observed service improvements on the Chicago-Detroit route where new Turboliners were operating, it discovered deficient or antiquated equipment on certain long-haul trains. For example, a 1976 Broadway Limited ride was found "extremely rough; sleeping car accommodations were soiled and stained and infested with rodents; and coaches were very old and in many instances lacked functioning restrooms, water fountains, air-slide doors, seats, interior lights, and heating or air conditioning."

Because of usually sufficient capacity, the ICC exempted some Amtrak trains from its regulations guaranteeing passengers reserved coach seats and food and beverages. Other exemptions dealt with mandatory station hours, availability of checked baggage service, and provision of sleeping cars on the Pioneer and Inter-American. The Amtrak Improvement Act of 1975 empowered the passenger carrier to discontinue trains without ICC involvement.

Beginning in 1977, Amtrak ceased absorbing the cost of air transportation furnished passengers missing connections due to late train arrivals. (Some of this lateness arose from the Federal Railroad Administration's having issued a slow order on 150 problem-ridden locomotives.)

An example of ICC enforcement was an action the agency brought in federal court against, *inter alia*, the Terminal Railroad Association of St. Louis. The suit was instituted to guarantee St. Louis passengers continued service in the face of redevelopment of that city's landmark station.

As the 1970s passed, Amtrak gained total or partial stock control over certain of its key stations, *viz.*, Chicago and Washington, as well as PC's Northeast Corridor.

3. Reports to Congress on the Rail Passenger Service Act
   (U.S. Department of Transportation, 1973 ff.)

Acting pursuant to the Amtrak Improvement Act of 1972, the secretary of transportation performed evaluations of the passenger carrier's early years of service. This process involved examining numerous aspects of its operation.

One of the areas studied was late running. As expected, long-haul trains with their greater exposure to equipment and track problems experienced the highest incidences of delay. In the three-year period 1971-73, on-time arrival of such trains was recorded at 56, 53, and 31 percent, respectively. An audit of Penn Central (PC) revealed that significant numbers of trains recorded by the carrier as arriving at destinations on time were, in fact, late. Illinois Central Gulf, with the "worst on-time record...for short-haul trains," was forced in an arbitration proceeding to restore its tracks to the condition prevailing on May 1, 1971, the Amtrak start-up date.

In assembling trains with cars acquired from diverse private carriers, Amtrak often experienced problems (lack of spare parts, wiring diagrams, etc.) when such equipment needed repairs at locations other than on the original owners' lines. Some relief was foreseen, however, with a plan to centralize heavy repairs at the former PC shop in Beech Grove, Indiana.

Because of the deteriorated condition of a number of locomotives, Amtrak deemed it prudent to assign extra units to minimize the impact of en route failures. This solution was not inexpensive, however, as fuel and mileage-related maintenance for one extra unit assigned to a 1,000-mile run was costing Amtrak about $485,000 annually. (The company then regarded an average car-to-locomotive ratio of 3:1 as normal.)

In October 1971, Amtrak consolidated the several previously independent Chicago passenger reservation bureaus into a single office. It also eliminated over one hundred separate railroad tariffs "of varying shapes and sizes." Similarly, in 1972 all then-existing Chicago commissaries were centralized at the former PC facility, now expanded.

Amtrak established a program to fill as many positions as feasible with its own employees. Such an approach was believed a solution to problems associated with divided loyalty and remote managerial control. One immediate saving arose from elimination of interline account settlements.

The company created the position of train director, largely filled by former dining car stewards. These individuals exercised supervision over all on-board services. Such approach supplanted an earlier program in which female service representatives rode selected trains to provide amenities to passengers.

Changes were also made in dining car operation, wherein meats prepared in microwave ovens replaced on-board butchering. Moreover, Amtrak negotiated new work rules allowing more flexible crew assignments, *e.g.*, individual employees may function on successive trips as bartender, coach attendant, etc.

By early 1972, a sales force of 149 people was deployed in twenty-seven cities. In addition, 5,300 domestic and foreign travel agents were appointed Amtrak representatives, of which 1,200 maintained ticket stock.

Amtrak was then moving mail in twelve markets nationwide and was preparing to extend this traffic to eight others. Further mail movements were seen as more difficult to obtain, however, because postal needs (frequently requiring evening arrivals, allowing overnight sorting prior to delivery) were deemed incompatible with many passengers' desires for morning arrivals. Amtrak also asserted that express shipments provided significant profit.

The 1972 legislation directed DOT to evaluate any changes in the composition of Amtrak's network that might seem appropriate. Accordingly, DOT surveyed the route structure, using the original criteria discussed in subchapter 1. Based upon calculations suggesting excessive unprofitability, DOT recommended elimination of these services:

(1) Chicago-Houston

(2) Chicago-Florida

(3) Richmond-Newport News

(4) New York/Washington-Kansas City

(5) Washington-Parkersburg

Following enactment of the Amtrak Improvement Act of 1973, calling for DOT designation of certain experimental routes to be operated for a period not less than two years, the secretary nominated, *e.g.*, Boston-Chicago and Norfolk-Cincinnati. The legislation also removed regulatory barriers imposed by states, notably California, that had precluded operation of "auto-ferry" trains. Such service was never implemented on the West Coast, however, because increased ridership on the only long-distance train—the Coast Starlight—consumed all available capacity.

Interestingly, in letters dated May 9, 1974, to the president of the Senate and Speaker of the House of Representatives, DOT Secretary Claude S. Brinegar complained that the 1973 amendment "substantially decreased the stewardship role of the Executive Branch" by removing his authority to attach terms and conditions to Amtrak grants.

4. Adequacy of Intercity Rail Passenger Service
   (Interstate Commerce Commission, 1973-76)

At the time of Amtrak's start-up, Congress authorized the Interstate Commerce Commission (ICC) to prescribe regulations for the adequacy of all intercity rail passenger service. Accordingly, the agency initiated an investigation proceeding (*Ex Parte* No. 277). At the outset, it dismissed challenges to its jurisdiction made by Amtrak, the Department of Transportation, and the Association of American Railroads. Additionally, it rejected an argument that reimbursement to passengers of monies paid in advance for services never actually received would constitute an illegal rebate.

Following its investigation, the ICC published regulations covering a wide range of passenger matters at 49 C.F.R. 1124. (It did, however, grant the carriers' request that special trains operated by them outside the nationwide system be exempted.) To include comment here on each of these regulations, most of them mundane, would unduly lengthen this volume. Nevertheless, the author believes that certain key provisions are worthy of mention, insofar as they dealt either with the kinds of relief ordered in situations where passengers would not likely have been cognizant of their rights, or with unexpected arguments by Amtrak in contesting certain of the regulations.

One hypothetical application of the regulations referred to an intermodal passenger traveling by train from Clifton Forge, Virginia, to Charleston, West Virginia, with the intent of flying from that point to Columbus, Ohio. Because a late train caused the passenger to miss the last airplane of the day, Amtrak was obliged to provide food and shelter at Charleston until the next available plane or bus departed for Columbus.

Applying even in circumstances beyond Amtrak's control, a regulation provided that passengers holding boarding reservations at "up-route" stations must be notified of cancelled trains. Amtrak objected to this requirement, claiming that the passengers usually resided an easy distance from the station and could therefore simply return home. The ICC, finding no justification for such an assertion, rebuffed Amtrak's argument.

Amtrak also challenged a regulation providing for the cleanliness of sleeping cars. The ICC quickly disposed of the question, stating that health and safety concerns are not subject to exemption.

To help passengers file complaints, both with individual carriers and with the ICC itself, the agency ordered that blank forms be made available on trains and in stations. Upon receipt of a complaint, operating carriers were required to respond within an allotted time or otherwise be deemed in default. The ICC stated that carriers should not be allowed to use safety issues as a shield against penalties for failure to honor their performance contracts with Amtrak.

The national "energy crisis" of the mid-1970s resulted in crowding on many trains. One effect was an increase in the number of passengers making reservations but not actually purchasing tickets, thus depriving Amtrak of revenue from potential customers denied passage. For example, first class space on Metroliner No. 103 was reported sold out for thirteen days in November 1974; yet the train experienced an average first class load factor of only 51 percent because of "no-shows." Moreover, the ICC cited instances wherein trains had unused capacity for extended portions of their runs because short-distance passengers occupied seats that otherwise could have been held for long-distance travelers. The agency reacted to the situation by allowing Amtrak to deny seat reservations to passengers traveling less than 200 miles.

Five months after institution of these regulations, the ICC declared that it was "less than pleased with the response...received from Amtrak" and was preparing "to act quickly in readying cases for court adjudication where informal means fail." One example of noncompliance concerned passengers on a 300-person train being forced to stand for an hour awaiting a place in a 36-seat dining car.

With the Amtrak Improvement Act of 1973, Congress conferred upon the ICC jurisdiction over the tracks employed in passenger service. In implementing this regulation, the agency broadened its ongoing investigation to consider requiring that (1) tracks used by Amtrak trains be maintained at a "level of utility" sufficient to allow retention of the elapsed times between terminals that prevailed in 1971,[29] and (2) certain short-haul corridor routes be evaluated for possible high-speed operation. Accordingly, it directed the operating carriers to indicate the then-existing status of their passenger lines and to identify the capital and other costs required to meet requirements imposed by the Federal Railroad Administration for various classes of upgraded track.

Ultimately, however, the ICC noted that as specified by operating agreements between Amtrak and its contracting railroads, the question of level of utility was being addressed by the National Arbitration Panel (NAP). That body had already ruled that two carriers, Illinois Central Gulf and Penn Central, had wrongfully allowed their passenger tracks to deteriorate. Amtrak vociferously informed the ICC that it believed other carriers had also done so, despite the private railroads uniformly (except Rock Island, a non-Amtrak carrier) having denied it.

Nevertheless, concluding that Amtrak could likely continue to prevail in NAP proceedings, the ICC saw no immediate need to grant Amtrak administrative relief other than for routes not covered by an operating agreement, *e.g.*, Texas and Pacific's Texarkana-Fort Worth line. Although the agency took receipt of the railroads' track upgrading estimates, it deferred promulgation of standards in this area pending completion of the ongoing rehabilitation of the Northeast Corridor, where the high-speed rail effort was then being concentrated.

In 1975, the ICC held twenty-four days of nationwide hearings to gauge the effectiveness of its published regulations. It took testimony from 308 public witnesses, as well as from Amtrak, several contracting railroads, and its own staff. The bulk of the testimony dealt with passenger complaints of all kinds relative to past Amtrak journeys. The state of Michigan, which was exercising an active role in improving service, made operational suggestions such as extending to Chicago the New York-Detroit run of the Empire State Express.

Based upon the hearing record, the presiding administrative law judge recommended certain revisions to the regulations. Although many were noncontroversial, the ICC rejected some, *e.g.*, a proposal to furnish passengers with blankets on selected trains.

---

[29] A level-of-utility clause appeared in Section 4.2 of the standard operating agreement between Amtrak and the freight railroads.

[Congress later repealed the statute under which the passenger service regulations had been prescribed. Nevertheless, readers wishing to research this area of the law will discover an abundance of background material, including passengers' first-hand experiences with Amtrak, in the several reports that were published: 334 I.C.C. 758 (1973), 346 I.C.C. 75 (1974), 346 I.C.C. 807 (1974), 348 I.C.C. 518 (1976), 351 I.C.C. 883 (1976), 352 I.C.C. 424 (1976).]

5. Reports of Special Subcommittee (House of Representatives, 1974-75)

[Under instructions from Interstate and Foreign Commerce Committee Chairman Harley O. Staggers of West Virginia, a special subcommittee* prepared reports covering operation of three Amtrak trains. (None of these trains exists today, although Amtrak continues to serve, with other trains, some of the stations.) An abstract of each of the three reports follows.]

* (Special Subcommittee on Investigations of the Committee on Interstate and Foreign Commerce, Ninety-third and Ninety-fourth Congress)

A. The Blue Ridge

In September 1971, Amtrak reinstated a portion of a daytime train once operated by the Baltimore and Ohio Railroad (B&O). Named the Potomac Special, the new service ran between Washington, D.C., and Parkersburg, West Virginia. It handled conventional cars, except during a three-month period in 1972 when turbo equipment was assigned. Power deficiencies demonstrated that the latter was not suited to the hilly topography characteristic of much of this line.

In March 1973, the Department of Transportation (DOT) recommended that the route be terminated because of disappointing ridership. [See subchapter 3.] Instead, however, the train was renamed the Blue Ridge and limited to operation east of Cumberland, Maryland, but with the expectation that Amtrak would discontinue it entirely on June 30, 1973. Negotiations begun by the states of Maryland and West Virginia to subsidize the train were halted when the Amtrak Improvement Act of 1973 provided for its continuation at least until June 30, 1974.

After analyzing the circumstances surrounding the Blue Ridge, the subcommittee recommended the train should not only be retained, but that it should be extended beyond Cumberland to Pittsburgh. It noted that Amtrak's other trains running between Washington and Pittsburgh en route to and from the Midwest (the daily Broadway Limited and the triweekly National Limited, both operating circuitously via Harrisburg) were scheduled for Pittsburgh stops at inconvenient hours and required a longer transit time than B&O had needed on its direct route via Cumberland before the Amtrak start-up.

Amtrak had originally rejected B&O for Washington-Pittsburgh service because severe track curvature required specially suspended cars to avoid side-swiping of passing trains, and because there was no direct connection at Pittsburgh with the east-west service operated over Penn Central (PC). The subcommittee observed, however, that B&O-owned cars fitted with the special suspensions would have been available for Amtrak's use and that eastbound passengers traveling to Washington (by then finding the Harrisburg-route trains chronically late) could easily transfer to the B&O line upon installation of a relatively simple track connection near PC's Pittsburgh station.

As for the Blue Ridge, Amtrak's position on manning assignments was to defer to B&O's labor contracts calling for a crew change at Brunswick, Maryland. Although the unions expressed willingness to consider an interdivisional crew, they conditioned it upon a modification of pay computation rules so that conductors' overtime would begin after the first 100 miles (the factor already applicable to engineers), rather than the then-existing 150 miles. For fear that a precedent unfavorable to management's options elsewhere might be set, B&O declined to go along. In this connection, the subcommittee pointed out that since the union leadership had indicated it would limit such a contract modification to the Washington-Cumberland line, Amtrak should not have meekly yielded to B&O's decision in the matter.

The subcommittee also analyzed 1973 accounting records by which B&O and the Washington Terminal Company had charged the Blue Ridge for locomotive fuel, car cleaning, equipment repairs, supplies, and administrative expenses. It discovered a large number of instances wherein Blue Ridge billings should have been made against the George Washington, a Washington-Cincinnati train operated for Amtrak by B&O's parent company, the Chesapeake and Ohio Railway. In another probe of 1973 accounts, the subcommittee questioned the correctness of nineteen monkey wrenches charged to the Blue Ridge in May and thirty-four more in June (when in other months there were few or none), along with precisely the same number each of hammers, air hoses, chisels, chains, coupler knuckles, and water jugs charged in both May and June. Additionally, the subcommittee discovered that B&O had charged the Blue Ridge for pension accruals covering employees ineligible for future pensions.

With the cutback of the train from Parkersburg to Cumberland, the subcommittee noted that on weekdays it had effectively become a commuter service. As such, it no longer required the deficit-producing buffet car, which by then was dispensing little more than "nonessential libations." Additionally, the subcommittee saw no further need for maintaining a ticket agent in Cumberland, since most passengers boarded at points east thereof where B&O operated an extensive commuter service to Washington and Baltimore.

The subcommittee observed that statistical studies underlying DOT's recommendation for discontinuance had failed to include data applicable to a more recent period of passenger growth. It also deplored an earlier Amtrak policy whereby the Blue Ridge equipment was "dead-headed" on Friday evenings from Cumberland back to Washington to position it for Saturday and Sunday round-trips to Harpers Ferry National Park, a Civil War site on the route. Thus, Amtrak forfeited revenue otherwise available for that dead-head movement, as well as for a similar one returning to Cumberland on Sunday evenings.

B. The National Limited

In March 1973, the Department of Transportation (DOT) had recommended that the National Limited, operating between New York/Washington and Kansas City, be discontinued because of purported low ridership and the prospect of continuing large deficits. [See subchapter 3.] In this connection, the subcommittee pointed out that DOT's *pro forma* projection of thirty-four average number of passengers on board was imprudently predicated upon initial low traffic counts taken during the first seven months of the train's start-up under Amtrak. Instead, the average passenger count had risen to fifty-four and ninety-one for the full years 1972 and 1973, respectively, and the train's loss per passenger-mile was declining.

In fact, in July 1973 (the month in which discontinuance was formally proposed) the National Limited experienced an operating profit. Referring to Amtrak's disclosure of letters it had received from the public in the last half of 1973, the subcommittee noted, "It appears paradoxical that the only train receiving more praises than criticisms was the National...." Indeed, the move to discontinue was abandoned in August 1973, a month after it was announced.

Perhaps some of the praises lavished upon the National Limited were undeserved. The train arrived late 100 percent of the time at both its New York and Kansas City terminals during the entire period November 1973-March 1974. This lateness undoubtedly resulted in considerable additional operating costs for extra passenger services provided and for increased overtime wages.

The subcommittee reported that an Amtrak audit of the Missouri Pacific (MP) portion of the recorded expenses applicable to the first eight months of operation revealed erroneous overpayments aggregating 3.5 percent of the total amounts billed. In addition, MP charged $23,400 to cover the salary of an operating officer during a period in which he performed no Amtrak-related work, but rather simply familiarized himself with the duties of that carrier's passenger superintendent in preparation for the latter's retirement. Moreover, while the gentleman was collecting this salary, it was known that he himself would reach the company's compulsory retirement age only seven months after being promoted.

Finally, the subcommittee discovered that at the St. Louis station, Amtrak was being charged excessive amounts for steam and hot water delivered through defective pipes characterized as "extremely old" and having "several leaks."

C. The Inter-American

In June 1972, Congress provided funds specifically for initiating rail passenger service between the U.S. and Mexico. (Later, the Amtrak Improvement Act of 1974 required establishment of on-board customs' inspection procedures to facilitate the most rapid possible through train movement.) Although Congress foresaw a new long-distance train, a general desire for quick inauguration of service led initially to Amtrak's creating in January 1973 a short-haul train connecting the border city of Laredo with Fort Worth, a station on the route of the Chicago-Kansas City-Houston Texas Chief. In March 1974, the Inter-American began operating between Chicago and Laredo, via St. Louis and Little Rock.

The subcommittee suggested that Amtrak management had worked to frustrate cross-border service of both the Inter-American and a National Railways of Mexico train, the Aztec Eagle. Relative to a Mexican proposal that through cars from its train cross into the U.S., an internal Amtrak memorandum at the vice-presidential level (possibly revealing an ulterior motive) stated, "It may be possible to gracefully put this idea to rest if the cars fail to meet either FRA [Federal Railroad Administration] or Amtrak standards. If this were the case, I think the pressure for through car operations would die for a long time to come."[30]

The Missouri Pacific Railroad (MP) had operated a passenger train on the St. Louis-Texarkana portion of the Inter-American route immediately before the Amtrak start-up. Between such points, that earlier train—making more stops than Amtrak's revived operation—consumed nine hours and forty-five minutes, or one hour and five minutes *less* than the running time MP insisted upon for Amtrak. No deterioration in the level of utility had occurred on MP's line, although the railroad had removed some track superelevation. However, by now MP had equalized the maximum speeds of freight and passenger trains through a reduction in the latter by 30 m.p.h. below that authorized by the FRA. Because of the

---

[30] For years, MP handled through St. Louis-Mexico City sleeping cars in its Sunshine Special or Texas Eagle trains.

Inter-American's slow schedule, same-day connections were missed southbound with the Aztec Eagle (operating from Nuevo Laredo, on the south bank of the Rio Grande River, to Mexico City) and northbound with Amtrak's National Limited (to Kansas City).

Contrastingly with MP, the subcommittee noted that the Atchison, Topeka and Santa Fe Railway (ATSF)—which handled the Inter-American between Fort Worth and Temple—allowed passenger operations at higher speeds than those for its freight trains and at the same speeds once authorized for its pre-Amtrak passenger trains. The subcommittee urged Amtrak not to use MP's lowered speeds as a base for establishing incentive payments covering on-time arrivals, as contemplated in a forthcoming renegotiation of its contract with that railroad.

Relative to the long-haul route finally selected by Amtrak for the Inter-American, the subcommittee identified three segments where it believed an alternate routing might have been preferable:

(1) Texarkana and Dallas—The subcommittee favored use of St. Louis Southwestern Railway (SSW)/Missouri-Kansas-Texas Railroad (MKT) joint handling. These carriers possess a shorter route with greater intermediate populations, although some amount of capital investment would have been required since no passenger service had been operated for years.

(2) Forth Worth and Temple—The subcommittee favored MKT via Waco because of "a large transient population from the universities which were not considered in Amtrak's calculations."

(3) Temple and Taylor—The subcommittee favored MKT tracks to obviate a time-consuming "dogleg" via Milano (an ATSF-MP junction), thus reducing the distance between such points by forty miles, *i.e.*, from seventy-nine to thirty-nine miles.[31]

According to the subcommittee's report, the Inter-American experienced an extraordinary number of air conditioning unit failures, some severe enough to necessitate passenger evacuation. These units operated on the principle whereby water was sprayed over Freon running through coils. Because of slow train speed, it was common for the water to evaporate in the intense Texas heat before cooling became effective, and for the axlebelt-driven generators to fail in keeping the batteries charged. Other battery failures arose from lack of charging facilities during the 13-hour layover at Laredo. Moreover, because of a variety of car voltage systems, it was frequently not possible to "jump-wire" the electrical system between adjacent cars to overcome battery problems.

---

[31] Amtrak ultimately adopted the MKT routing (now Union Pacific) between Temple and Taylor. Currently, the timetable indicates a distance of 38 miles.

Finally, the subcommittee found fault with Amtrak's station planning. Reportedly, a costly delay had ensued in constructing four powered turnouts at Little Rock. There was also a belief that the Texas and Pacific Railway had overcharged Amtrak for installing a wye at Fort Worth. At San Antonio, Amtrak initially could find no feasible spot for a permanent station other than a site five miles from the central business district, and hence opposed by the city's chamber of commerce. No station building was planned for San Marcos, location of Aquarena Springs, characterized as one of the "most popular commercial attractions" in Texas. At Austin, MP permitted Amtrak to occupy only about one-third of the space (allowing for just sixteen seats) in the station once used for its own passenger service.

6. Report to Congress on the Amtrak Route System
   (U.S. Department of Transportation, 1979)

Following several years of increasing deficits, Congress enacted the Amtrak Improvement Act of 1978. It called for the Department of Transportation (DOT) to make recommendations for "an optimal intercity railroad passenger system, based upon current and future market and population requirements...." These recommendations were intended to identify the end points of routes in any restructured network, the quality of service appropriate for the various routes, and the anticipated revenues and expenses. The statute directed DOT to give consideration to the unique characteristics and advantages of rail service, energy conservation, cost-benefit relationships, availability of alternate transportation, and the impact of demand upon service frequency and fare structures.

Before considering prospective route changes, DOT commented upon several passenger service matters. The agency was critical of Amtrak's USA Rail Pass, sold for unlimited travel during a given period at a fixed price, on the ground that it diluted the revenue yield by offering a discount to travelers willing to pay a higher price for full-fare tickets. Also, DOT not only specifically criticized Interstate Commerce Commission (ICC) regulations requiring Amtrak to provide sufficient equipment to handle peak demand, it was instrumental in Congress's wiping out all of the regulations protecting passenger rights.

The first step in DOT's route-examination process was to define five "system concepts," *i.e.*, five alternate levels of operations ranging from very limited day service radiating from a few large metropolitan centers, to an expansive service comprising basically the then-current system augmented by the addition of many interregional and intraregional links.

Of the five concepts, DOT decided upon a middle approach incorporating a combination of short-distance corridors and a single east-west service, intersected by a few north-south services on both coasts and in the interior. Accordingly, on May 1, 1978, DOT presented a preliminary plan embracing the above principles. Not all such services would operate daily, however. [Certain corridor routes are omitted from the discussion here.]

In the East, two trains would run from New York to serve both coasts of Florida, one each via Columbia and Charleston. A Boston-Chicago service would operate via Cleveland, and a service from New York would split at Pittsburgh, with sections to Chicago and St. Louis/Kansas City. Washington would be linked both with New Orleans via Atlanta and with Chicago via Charlottesville and Cincinnati. Chicago would be connected to St. Louis and New Orleans. Stub operations would run New York-Montréal via Springfield, and Chicago-Detroit.

In the West, there would be a single route from Chicago via Minneapolis to Seattle/Portland, with a stub to Duluth. Chicago-California service would consist of a line via Albuquerque to Barstow, having a stub from La Junta to Denver, and separate sections to Oakland and Los Angeles. There would also be a line from Chicago to Houston via Topeka and Forth Worth, and a line from New Orleans to Los Angeles. Finally, on the West Coast there would be a Seattle-Los Angeles line.

The statute ordering the DOT study also directed a unit of the ICC, *viz.*, its Rail Services Planning Office (RSPO), to conduct hearings enabling the public to comment upon the proposed restructuring. Fifty-two such hearings (under *Ex Parte* No. 351) were held in large and small communities across the nation, but generally in areas directly affected. In addition, RSPO allowed interested persons to submit written comments. Altogether, 4,200 persons or entities participated in the process. Aside from bus operators and certain rail freight carriers, most were not in favor of the DOT proposal.

For example, Governor Dixie Lee Ray of Washington complained that since no savings were being projected in Amtrak's overhead expenses, the entire amount would then be spread over the remaining trains and thus worsen their financial positions. Congressman Teno Roncalio testified that the Wyoming Highway Patrol had closed Interstate 80 (a road paralleling the route of the San Francisco Zephyr) twelve times during the preceding winter because of snow and high winds, and that the Federal Aviation Administration closes the Cheyenne airport a total of about thirty days every winter, with each closure normally lasting two to three days. The state of North Carolina emphasized that rather than promote a system capable of meeting future needs, DOT had dwelled excessively upon "near-term solutions." Other witnesses accused DOT of an antirail bias and of concocting a system to fit an arbitrary subsidy level.

In its analysis of the preliminary report, RSPO emphasized that Congress had replaced the "for profit" objective with "social and environmental criteria" as the appropriate methodology for evaluating

Amtrak's route structure. Thus, RSPO concluded that it was essential for DOT to adopt the latter approach in its upcoming final report. RSPO also observed that DOT's reliance upon fully allocated costs (reflecting reservation/information systems, maintenance facilities, advertising, etc.) produced a "meaningless measure for reviewing the performance of individual routes...." Moreover, RSPO noted the U.S. General Accounting Office had previously found that Amtrak's Route Profitability System (which DOT had used) "is not presently designed to estimate the costs that would be saved if a train or route were discontinued or their frequencies reduced." RSPO stated that because of faulty DOT estimating procedures, projections of improved financial performance expected from the remaining trains (presumed to arise from a transfer to such trains of some passengers disaccommodated from the discontinued services) might not materialize and a restructured system could result in requiring the same level of federal appropriation, but provide "less service to fewer people."

In its final report dated January 31, 1979 (which, by statute, would be automatically implemented on October 1, 1979, unless exigencies of some kind were to intervene), DOT's revised network proposal reflected a 43 percent reduction in Amtrak's route-miles. That final report was considerably different from the preliminary one in many significant respects.

Thus, in the East the Boston-Chicago train would now run via Detroit, with "closed doors" while in Canada. New York-Chicago and Washington-Chicago service would operate on a consolidated basis via Pittsburgh and Cleveland. Chicago to St. Louis and New Orleans, as well as the New York-Florida service, appeared unchanged from the preliminary report.

In the West, the earlier proposed Chicago-Seattle service remained, but without the Duluth stub. From Chicago to California, DOT had made a major change: The Southwest Limited and California Zephyr would be consolidated to operate via Kansas City, Denver, and Ogden, where it would split to serve both Oakland and Los Angeles (the latter a new service through Las Vegas). Trains from both Seattle and New Orleans to Los Angeles appeared unchanged from the preliminary report.

DOT's final report earmarked nineteen long-distance trains for elimination on October 1, 1979 (although on some routes alternate Amtrak service would remain for a portion or all of the distance). They are listed below in the order of appearance in the report:

(1) Inter-American, Chicago-St. Louis-Laredo.

(2) Southwest Limited (La Junta-Barstow portion).

(3) Broadway Limited (Pittsburgh-Chicago portion).

(4) Lake Shore Limited (Buffalo-Chicago portion).

(5) San Francisco Zephyr (Chicago-Denver portion).

(6) Pioneer, Salt Lake City-Seattle.

(7) National Limited, New York/Washington-Kansas City.

(8) Montréaler, Washington-Montréal.

(9) Silver Meteor, New York-Miami.

(10) Champion, New York-St. Petersburg.

(11) Cardinal, Washington-Charlottesville-Chicago.

(12) Hilltopper, Washington-Petersburg-Chicago.

(13) North Coast Hiawatha, Chicago-Seattle.

(14) Lone Star, Chicago-Houston.

(15) Southern Crescent, New York-New Orleans

(16) Floridian, Chicago-St. Petersburg/Miami

(17) San Joaquin, Bakersfield-Oakland.

(18) Mount Ranier, Seattle-Portland.

(19) Pacific International, Vancouver-Seattle.

While a number of the proposed train discontinuances were implemented on October 1, 1979, in accordance with DOT's final report, some were not. [32]

DOT next analyzed the financial ramifications. For the fiscal year 1980 then beginning, the agency estimated the amount for continuing the existing service at $949 million ($718 million operating and $231 million capital, respectively). Using the curtailed network in the DOT final report, the comparable figure was projected at $760 million ($552 million oper-

---

[32] Of the trains slated for discontinuance on October 1, 1979, six (National Limited, Champion, Hilltopper, Floridian, North Coast Hiawatha, and Lone Star) were eliminated on that date; others lasted longer, and some continue to the date of this writing.

ating and $208 million capital). According to DOT, the 1980 savings would therefore be the difference, or $189 million. [33]

7. Evaluation of Service to Areas Not Presently Served (Amtrak, 1992)

The Amtrak Reauthorization and Improvement Act of 1990 directed the passenger carrier to evaluate the economic feasibility of entering new markets having the potential of recouping their associated operating costs. Accordingly, Amtrak divided the continental United States into four regions (West, Midwest, East, and South) and selected for study between two and four routes from each. These selections included two western "rural service routes" in sparsely populated territory.

For consideration in the study, Amtrak determined that a potential route must (1) link major population clusters with important regional centers, tourist attractions, or state capitals then without service; (2) extend present routes to serve additional populated areas; (3) comprise a logical link in the current network; or (4) establish short-distance connectors to feed riders from moderately sized communities to existing long-distance services.

Based upon the above criteria, Amtrak identified twenty possible new routes, some of which having previously been considered for adoption. For each, it developed ridership and revenue projections through application of an econometric model calibrated from market responses to various service patterns observed over the preceding two decades. The model was sensitive to considerations of population, travel time and distance, service frequency, and times of day that stations are served. Also, each route was analyzed for its potential for postal contracts.

In projecting costs, Amtrak used past engineering field surveys, new studies, or judgments based upon prior experience in similar territories. In a few instances, it found that rails, ties, ballast, etc., would need to be upgraded. Some lines carrying high-density freight service would require installation of passing sidings at locations where the terrain allowed. Special locomotives would be needed on lines equipped for inductive cab signal devices. Capital costs were estimated for stations and platforms, crew quarters, pollution control facilities, storage tracks, standby power, potable water connections, and grade crossing and signal modifications. Crew expenses reflected prevailing labor contracts and practices. Costs

---

[33] It is arresting that while DOT claimed elimination of all nineteen trains would reduce the fiscal 1980 operating subsidy by $166 million ($718 million minus $552 million), actual discontinuance of the six trains shown in the previous footnote reduced it by only $1.1 million ($718 million minus the $716.9 million audited deficit reported for that year by the General Accounting Office in, for example, page 28 of GAO/RCED-95-71). In other words, to achieve an annual saving to the U.S. government of $1.1 million, the country lost 100 percent of its rail passenger service to Columbus, Dayton, Louisville, Nashville, Montgomery, Oklahoma City, and scores of other places.

developed in the study were adjusted, where necessary, to reflect 1992-level dollars.

Estimates of incremental subsidy and passenger-miles per train-mile or PM/TM (average number of passengers on board) for the twenty routes studied, separated by short- and long-distance services, are depicted in Table 2 in ascending order of subsidy:

Table 2
Estimated Subsidy and Ridership of Possible New Trains

	Incremental Subsidy (000)	PM/TM
Short-Distance Services		
(1) Minneapolis-Kansas City	($835)-$926*	39-59
(2) Extend St. Louis-Kansas City Mule to Omaha	($993)-$14*	84-94
(3) New York-Harrisburg via Allentown	($1,110)-(860)	87-102
(4) Chicago-Madison	($1,534)-(605)	55-83
(5) Chicago-Green Bay	($2,679)-($1,687)	43-64
(6) Vancouver-Portland	($2,961)-($2,626)	82-101
(7) Boston-Portland	($3,388)	54
Long-Distance Services		
(8) Extend Sunset Ltd. to Miami	($1,119)	182
(9) Cleveland to Cincinnati	($2,373)	233
(10) Chicago-Dallas via Oklahoma (triweekly)	($3,285)	282
(11) Jacksonville-New Orleans (daily)	($6,099)	91
(12) Chicago-Dallas via Okla. (daily)	($8,443)	153
(13) New York-Atlanta via Tenn.	($9,624)-($7,896)	62-72
(14) Denver-Dallas	($11,502)-($8,292)	94-156
(15) Vancouver-Los Angeles	($12,848)-($8,208)	205-250
(16) Reroute Pioneer/Desert Wind, Iowa & Wyoming	($14,171)	182
(17) Southern Montana leg-Empire Builder	($15,352)-($12,632)	152-163
(18) New York-Florida via Charlotte	($20,250)-($10,644)	276-307
(19) Chicago-Florida	($20,800)-($18,000)	131-194
(20) Denver-Spokane	($24,377)-($22,619)	49-73

* Two of these routes, Minneapolis-Kansas City and Omaha-Kansas City (an extension of the Mule), were forecast to require no subsidy at the upper end of the range of passengers shown. The higher figures—59 and 94, respectively—reflect through passengers connecting to/from the

California Zephyr at Chariton, Iowa (a new stop), and Omaha, Nebraska. The company noted that these counts would have been even higher were it not for the Zephyr's capacity limitation.

Amtrak observed that closing gaps in its route structure would create numerous origin and destination possibilities and, thereby, offer a widened transportation choice to many Americans.

Chapter III
How Do Amtrak's Competitors Measure Up?

It became clear during Amtrak's first twenty-five years that whenever a discussion ensues relative to the best means of channeling the nation's intercity transportation resources, someone is going to claim that highway and air infrastructures can satisfy virtually all known demand. And surely, these modes have benefited from marvelous technological advances. But an analysis of news accounts and other sources makes it clear that they suffer critical shortcomings.

At the outset, we should recognize that some of our respected opinion-makers and congressional leaders are concerned that fundamental transportation policies affecting modal use are predicated upon invalid premises. In an op-ed column appearing in *The Washington Post* of August 15, 1994, Jessica Mathews (a senior fellow at the Council on Foreign Relations and knowledgeable on worldwide transportation systems) observed a "great canard about Amtrak is that it alone requires a subsidy..." On July 28, 1995, the same newspaper reported Senator Robert C. Byrd of West Virginia as saying that of 14,000 votes he had cast during seven terms in office, he regretted only two of them, one being the vote to deregulate passenger airlines because in his eyes service to his home state had "deteriorated" as a result.

Later in this chapter, we shall discuss subsidies and air carrier deregulation in greater depth.

1. Highway Travel

    A. Limitations Arising from Congestion

The Ohio Turnpike is an east-west toll road traversing north-central Ohio. Although regarded as important to such medium-size Ohio cities as Youngstown and Akron, it also serves as a link in a multistate corridor connecting the Northeast and Midwest. Indeed, for most of its length it is designated Interstate 80.

In 1995, an increasing volume of turnpike traffic prompted highway authorities to approve construction of additional lanes. According to an official state publication (*Turnpike News*, February 29, 1996, Volume 2, Number 4), these new lanes were budgeted at over a half-billion dollars. Although Ohio taxpayers bear residual responsibility if tolls should prove inadequate to recover the amount of the expenditure, use of this artery by non-Ohioans makes the turnpike's management and financial situation matters of national interest.

In the same year in which Ohio committed itself to funding the added turnpike lanes, Amtrak responded to a systemwide cash flow problem by, in part, discontinuing completely the Pittsburgh-Chicago portion of its New York-Chicago Broadway Limited that also operated across north-central Ohio. The discontinued portion constituted the only Amtrak service connecting Youngstown and Akron (and other points) with the outside world.

In addition, this train was valuable to residents of Philadelphia (to name one large city on the Broadway Limited route as an example) because it had long offered them through sleepers and diner as well as coaches to/from the principal western rail gateway at Chicago. Amtrak's solution to the Philadelphians' plight was its Three Rivers, a coach-only train that began operating on the schedule of the former Broadway Limited east of Pittsburgh, but with the latter's dining and lounge facilities downgraded to "sandwich, snack, and beverage service." While the Three Rivers was timed to connect at Pittsburgh with the Washington-Cleveland-Chicago Capitol Limited (and thus offer a semblance of Philadelphia-Chicago service), Amtrak required eastbound passengers to change cars at 5:20 A.M.; westbound, such passengers would wait until 11:02 P.M. to change.[34]

From the standpoint of the wise allocation of the nation's resources devoted to the provision of transportation capacity, the question arises as to whether our governmental agencies are functioning at cross purposes. If any definitive economic studies were made to determine whether the available resources should be employed to fund the costly turnpike lane additions, or alternatively, provide the comparatively modest assistance necessary to maintain the parallel rail route, they have not come to this author's attention. Certainly, no one has asked whether he prefers increased highway tolls to higher fares or taxes sufficient to preserve the only train operating over the line.

If few people desired rail service, allowing demise of the Broadway Limited would perhaps have been understandable. But reports in the

---

[34] Later, through New York-Chicago coaches (but no sleepers) began operating on a combination of the Three Rivers and Capitol Limited, with switching between the two trains performed at Pittsburgh. Now the Three Rivers coaches are again handled over the Broadway Limited Route west of Pittsburgh, but they pass through Akron without stopping.

trade press, along with experiences related by acquaintances of this author, show that the Capitol Limited cannot always absorb all of the Philadelphians and others wishing to travel to/from Chicago. Similarly, reportedly sold-out trips of the Lake Shore Limited (another East Coast-Chicago train) may preclude the overflow from routing their journeys via New York City.

Experiencing a high level of frustration, many Philadelphia customers having to travel to Chicago likely resigned themselves to finding a nonrail (albeit less satisfactory) alternative. But let us hope reduced Amtrak ticket sales do not delude the company into thinking that public need for train service in this important market has declined.

North-central Ohio was not the only part of the nation where questionable decisions were made in 1995 concerning the prudent employment of transportation resources. Articles (May 11, 1995 and August 22, 1996) in *The Washington Post* reported that highway officials were planning to spend between $1-$3 billion in local and federal money to replace the Woodrow Wilson Bridge, an Interstate 95 draw span crossing the Potomac River to the south of Washington. Built in the 1960s to carry 75,000 vehicles per day, it was rapidly deteriorating from the 172,000 that by then were using it. (The count continues to grow.) Options ranged from a double-deck replacement bridge, which would overwhelm the ambience of nearby Alexandria's eighteenth century historical district, to a 12-lane tunnel.

In addition to the funds expended for bridging the river, highway authorities propose to budget up to $322 million for a single relocated interchange on the west bank and an unspecified sum on the east side "for one ramp [that] would cross an elementary school playground...." Even assuming that sufficient space remains at the school for such facilities as children's softball, one may speculate how the umpire would be heard over the traffic noise when calling balls and strikes, etc.

Highway I-95, connecting the Northeast with Florida, roughly parallels Amtrak's East Coast route. Like the fate of the Broadway Limited, in 1995 Amtrak discontinued its New York-Tampa Palmetto.[35] May we dare ask whether local communities should be forced to suffer the intrusive disruptions described above for the benefit of highway travelers on a route that once enjoyed abundant rail passenger service?[36]

---

[35] Although service was later restored on approximately the same schedule, Amtrak simultaneously withdrew its long-standing Silver Star trains from Tampa.

[36] Local traffic constitutes a significant portion of the vehicles crossing the Wilson Bridge. In yet another seemingly inexplicable situation, the regional public transit authority operates just three buses westbound across the bridge in the morning commuter rush period, and three eastbound in the late afternoon. None operates at other times. There are no known plans to expand bus service; indeed, virtually every bus line in the system has recently seen curtailed service, with some eliminated completely. Similarly, heavy rail transit is being selectively reduced also. These service reductions come at a time of worsening congestion on the area's streets.

In another part of the nation, the *Houston Chronicle* reported on April 2, 1995, that most of the portion of Interstate 35 within Texas "is functioning at or beyond its traffic-carrying capacity." Added truck traffic occasioned by the North American Free Trade Agreement would likely exacerbate the problem. From 1992 through the summer of 1994, the state of Texas spent $142 million on construction, reconstruction, and preventive maintenance on I-35; it plans to spend $342 million more in the next seven years. Nonlocal traffic on the segment between San Antonio and Austin, served by Amtrak's Texas Eagle, had increased 754 percent since 1960 to 49,000 vehicles per day.

Yet, in 1993 Amtrak reduced Eagle service from daily to triweekly. In 1995, it went further by discontinuing that train's Dallas-Houston stub. A year after that, the carrier proposed to eliminate all service south of St. Louis.

B. Reductions in Safety

In 1995, Congress gave the states flexibility in establishing their own maximum highway speed limits. According to *The Washington Post* of December 8th of that year, this action was taken despite the National Highway Traffic Safety Administration's having projected that in going from 55 to 65 m.p.h. on rural interstates, "6,400 more people would die every year and an extra $19 billion would be added in health care costs." In a November 18, 1995, op-ed article in the same newspaper, Colman McCarthy reported that the Department of Transportation "estimates that a third of the cost of motor vehicle injuries is paid by tax dollars."

In this author's opinion, there is a lot to be said for allowing persons to freely decide for themselves what risks they are willing to assume. Conversely, there appears little justification for forcing upon the remainder of the populace the concomitant costs resulting from such assumption. Our government not only requires those persons who choose not to assume the risks of highway misfortunes to nevertheless help pay the speeders' medical bills, it also has adopted transportation policies preventing Americans in all except a few markets from selecting a demonstrably safer form of surface travel, *i.e.*, railroads.

C. Noise Abatement Contrivances

An article in *The Washington Post* of July 24, 1995, quantified some of the costs that society bears in ameliorating highway noise. Specifically, it described walls of concrete, wood, metal, or fiberglass now lining highways carrying interstate traffic through suburban neighborhoods. Although the article was confined to the situation prevailing in Maryland and Virginia, such walls exist in many other states too.

The state of Maryland had by then spent $100 million of its allocated federal highway funds on noise abatement. Homes exposed to a level of sixty-seven decibels, equivalent to the sound emitted from a vacuum cleaner at ten feet, are eligible for a noise barrier installation costing up to $50,000. In Virginia, the comparable maximum limit per home is $30,000.

While federally assisted projects are commonly financed from the Highway Trust Fund, user taxes and fees channeled into this fund are typically insufficient to cover disbursements. Rep. John R. Kasich of Ohio has noted that for twelve of the past fifteen years, the federal government spent more from the fund than it collected in receipts. For example, in 1994 it spent $22 billion while collecting only $18 billion, leaving a deficiency of $4 billion. The situation worsened the next year. Sen. William V. Roth, Jr., of Delaware announced that for 1995, the deficiency nearly doubled to almost $8 billion.

D. Bus Alternatives

In its various attempts to justify a lessening of federal support for the maintenance of a national rail passenger network, the U.S. Department of Transportation (DOT) has usually extolled the availability of buses that generally parallel many Amtrak rail routes. So let us examine the reality of this alternative.

When most private intercity rail passenger operations ceased in May 1971, nearly 40 percent of the trains theretofore operated were not absorbed into the newly created Amtrak system. This exclusion presented the bus industry with an opportunity to capture the traffic previously handled on the omitted trains. Figures released by the Transportation Association of America in a July 1977 publication, *Transportation Facts and Trends*, show on page 22 the passenger-miles generated by bus patrons for a series of pertinent years.

Thus, in the last full year of private rail operation (1970), bus carriers reported 25.3 billion intercity passenger-miles. In Amtrak's first full year (1972), bus traffic accounted for 25.6 billion, an increase of only 1.2 percent. Although buses gained some ridership from the gasoline shortage experienced the following winter, by 1976 intercity bus passenger-miles had declined to 25.1 billion. As can be seen, such a level was below the pre-Amtrak ridership.

Why were buses not able to pick up the bulk of the former rail passengers? An article in *The New York Times* of December 9, 1974, gives us an insight: "Compared with other modes of travel, an intercity bus journey can be slow and bumpy and an interminable succession of stops." Consistent with the perception of buses as a relatively uncomfortable form of travel, a 1977 U.S. Senate study titled *Intercity Domestic Transportation System for Passengers and Freight* found at page 335 that the typical intercity bus offers its passengers an average of 5.6 square feet per passenger, or only 60-80 percent of that typically provided on a commercial airliner and one-third to one-sixth that provided on a train.

Reacting to a continuing decline in patronage, Greyhound Lines (the largest domestic carrier) began retrenching. A map in *The Washington Post* of February 20, 1986, identified thirty-five bus stations that the carrier was closing. About half of these were located in cities served by Amtrak.

Regulatory relief enacted by Congress in 1982, easing service and fare restrictions on bus firms in light of their loss of market share, neither revitalized the industry nor stemmed the decline in regular-route service. Indeed, after purchasing Trailways in 1987 in an effort to maximize efficiencies, Greyhound filed for bankruptcy protection in 1990. In a 1992 report (GAO/RCED-92-126), the U. S. General Accounting Office noted at page 16 that of 12,000 locations served by bus in 1982, fewer than 6,000 then remained. Most of the lost service was in rural areas not reached by air carriers.

In 1992, Greyhound ceased including its schedules in *Russell's Official National Motor Coach Guide* (Russell's Guides, Inc., Cedar Rapids, Iowa). Moreover, this carrier now rarely furnishes timetables to prospective or actual passengers requesting them. Neither are baggage windows still commonly placed inside terminals, leaving bus-side checking as the sole means of handling all except carry-on bags.

In the face of all of the bus industry's troubles, DOT nevertheless says that train passengers displaced by Amtrak discontinuances can switch to buses. To the extent that bus service has not disappeared on particular routes, perhaps they can. But we Americans should be honest enough to admit that the quality of common-carrier, surface transportation in the U.S. is heading toward third-world standards.

Even in Kenya (a country for which American tourists returning home are exempted from paying customs duties on souvenir purchases because of its status as a "developing" nation), this author enjoyed a 1991 overnight train journey from Nairobi to Mombasa that offered first class sleeping accommodations and dining car meals served on real china marked with the Kenya Railways logo. Similarly, a day trip the following week on the National Railways of Zimbabwe from Harare to Bulawayo featured real china with the NRZ logo. It is disconcerting to come home and see such services vanishing from the "only remaining world superpower" as we like to perceive ourselves.

2. Air Travel

In the sections below, we will be addressing some very serious concerns relative to the ability of air carriers to satisfactorily handle all of the needs of this country's citizens that some would place upon them. While deferring until later chapters a discussion as to the merits of rail subsidies, let us acknowledge here that there are people who have understandable reasons to find air service not in their interest. Some of them are well known individuals; as a result, their views have been noted in the public press.

An article in *The Washington Post* of July 28, 1990, observed that the entertainer Cher, having been on a plane that developed engine trouble, "is sticking to terra firma from now on and will travel by train and bus to concerts...." Moreover, the December 8, 1995, issue of the same newspaper reported that Christine Lavin—a member of an all-female singing group—labeled Boston's airport "Amtrak's Best Friend" after a computer malfunction there resulted in cancellation of a flight that would have taken her to perform in a concert.

Dick Young, a former sportswriter for the *New York Daily News*, has said, "Traveling was fun when teams played mostly in the daytime and went by train. Now you play a night game...whip out a story for deadline and then rush to catch the plane. The guy who makes up the baseball schedule is a sadist."

Additionally, John Madden, long associated with professional football as a coach and commentator, is known for going to great lengths in arranging surface transportation (including rail) when feasible.

With the above snippets serving as an introduction, let us now go to the heart of the matter.

A. Public Costs and Subsidies

An article in *The Washington Post* for April 1, 1995, seems to constitute as good a basis as any for beginning our discussion of the allocation of public funds to air transportation purposes. This article describes a mammoth airport proposed for construction in Northwestern Arkansas. The principal driving forces behind the project were three large, Arkansas-based national businesses. They are engaged in retail store operation, chicken processing, and motor truck haulage, respectively.

The local congressman first arranged a hearing to boost interest in replacing the existing small Fayetteville airport with a larger jet facility. Two months later, the Department of Transportation approved a $601,000 grant covering an airport study for which, surprisingly or not, no local entities had asked. The study suggested that Arkansas poultry producers could use the new airport, with two 12,500-foot runways, to reach an untapped Japanese market for fresh chicken. Similarly, ten jumbo jets per month could bring electronics and apparel from the Far East for distribution to U.S. stores nationwide. The general counsel of the chicken company reputedly told the study group that, "There is an incredible chance to get $90 million from the federal government...."

When, however, the Federal Aviation Administration (FAA) rejected a cargo airport, the local group shifted its emphasis to one designed for passengers. Thereupon, the FAA released $9 million for land acquisition and $12 million for site development.

Nevertheless, a consulting firm specializing in airport usage described the new plan as "a private interest boondoggle." Moreover, a spokesman for the Air Transport Association declared that the proposed facility would escalate airlines' costs of serving Fayetteville as much as five-fold. Two major airlines from which the boosters had solicited support were reportedly "lukewarm" at best.

If the airport development were halted at this point, the taxpayers could presumably restrict their losses to the $21.6 million already spent. Should the project continue forward, a terminal and single runway would soak up another $144 million.

Long-time observers of the rail passenger business will recognize Fayetteville as a point once served by trains of the former St. Louis-San Francisco Railway. Such trains connected with that carrier's Meteor and Texas Special to provide through service to/from points in Missouri, Kansas, Oklahoma, and Texas. One might speculate what the cost would be to reestablish rail service. The $165.6 million that could be squandered on this single airport is the equivalent of 19.4 percent of Amtrak's 1995 loss on its entire forty-five-state system.

But rather than spend more time on a proposal that may never be consummated, let us turn our attention to a new airport that actually was built, *viz.*, Denver International. An Associated Press dispatch reported that this $4.9 billion facility, opened in March 1995, is so costly a place in which to operate that the $35 million annual rent previously paid by United Airlines in Denver would increase to $210 million.

Moreover, a May 21, 1995, article in *The Denver Post* reported that while average air fares to forty major cities remained constant from April 1994 to April 1995, fares to Denver increased 20 percent. Ominously for the airlines—and for the taxpayers' investment—Denver passenger traffic declined 5.6 percent during this period. Between Denver and Grand Junction, Colorado, air traffic fell 28 percent. (One could ask how hard Amtrak has tried, if at all, to capitalize upon Coloradoans' disillusionment with their air service on this train-competitive route.)

Another airport expansion in the making is at St. Louis, an Amtrak hub of sorts. According to the *St. Louis Post-Dispatch* of July 16, 1995, airport officials there have sited a new runway location that will require seizing 1,500 homes and seventy businesses. The condemnation process, creating great anguish, is budgeted at $400 million and will involve razing one-third of the community of Bridgeton. (The article does not reveal what the other two-thirds feel about this development.)

On December 1, 1987, syndicated newspaper columnists Jack Anderson and Joseph Spear reported that the Essential Air Service subsidy program—designed to ease the perceived hardship inflicted upon rural communities by the Airline Deregulation Act—had gone "haywire." Big payments were being authorized on flights handling one or two passengers who could have used alternate air service available at a larger airport barely an hour's drive away.

These columnists cited specifically the situation in Manitowoc, Wisconsin, a city once served by Chicago and North Western Railway passenger trains. The average per trip cost of providing air service at such point, only thirty-nine miles from Green Bay and also seen as within reasonable driving distance of Milwaukee, was defrayed by the combination of an $89 passenger ticket and a whopping $515 taxpayer allowance.

In lieu of our looking at more repetitious examples of the lofty subsidies associated with air transportation, let us go now directly to a recent issue (*viz.*, fiscal year 1996) of the *Budget of the United States Government*. On page 711, we find the aviation account (Airport and Airway Trust Fund). Itemized therein are estimates for the various sources of "cash income": passenger ticket, waybill, fuel, and international departure taxes; intragovernment transactions; and miscellaneous collections. Offsetting the income are items of "cash outgo": FAA operations; airport grants-in-aid; facilities and equipment; research, engineering and development; rents; and payments to air carriers.

For 1996, the aviation account began with a balance of $12.0 billion. With estimated income of $6.8 billion and outgo of $6.7 billion, it was projected to end the year with a balance of $12.1 billion. On page 743, the FAA budget was portrayed in terms of "Budget Authority," "Obligations," and "Outlays." The total net funding for these three classifications was $6.9 billion, $7.0 billion, and $8.3 billion, respectively.

On page 748, the following statement appeared: "For 1996, it is proposed that $2,609,123,000 of the [FAA] operations appropriation be financed from the Trust Fund. This would provide an overall 75 percent cost recovery for FAA programs in total."

The corollary of the foregoing assertion is, of course, that the residual 25 percent of the cost of FAA's 1996 programs would not be recovered from monies paid by users into the air trust fund. In such regard, there appeared in *The Washington Post* for October 5, 1993, a letter to the editor by James E. Coston of Chicago, Illinois, in his then-capacity as a nominee to the Amtrak board of directors. Mr. Coston called attention to a 1988 Congressional Budget Office study which had found that for the period 1971-88, $54.9 billion of the FAA's budget (or 54.9 percent) was derived from the general fund, *i.e.*, such amount was not covered by user fees.

Before we end this section, it would be instructive to review a related matter, *viz.*, the question of lost revenue to the government arising through business travel deductions from income taxes. Testifying before the House of Representatives on March 14, 1985, Amtrak President W. Graham Claytor, Jr., noted that whereas only 20 percent of rail passengers are business travelers, 65 percent of air travelers fall into such category. The significance of the latter is $7 billion lost annually to the government in taxes not paid, a figure that equated to an indirect air subsidy of $33 per airline passenger.

B. Carrier Entry and Withdrawal from Markets

A search of Interstate Commerce Commission (ICC) reports from the 1960s era reveals that a common justification used in permitting passenger train discontinuances was prevalence of alternate air service. This author cannot recall an instance in which an ICC proceeding was reopened for reason that such air service itself was subsequently eliminated.[37] Nevertheless, communities of various sizes have discovered over the years that they do not necessarily retain the air option indefinitely.

In a December 18, 1970, article, *The Wall Street Journal* observed that Mohawk Airlines had dropped its late evening flight to Binghamton from New York, causing hardship to people seeking to return home at day's end from that east coast metropolis. At one time, the Delaware, Lackawanna and Western Railroad provided overnight New York-to-Binghamton service on its Owl train, scheduled for arrival at the beginning of the business day. Displaced air travelers no longer had the rail option.

Similarly, the same article noted that Ozark Airlines had removed all of its flights from Iowa City, Iowa. The latter point, on the main line of the former Chicago, Rock Island and Pacific Railroad, enjoyed through the 1950s four daily east-west trains in both directions. Travelers to and from Iowa City, a major medical center, then found themselves with neither trains nor planes.

A February 18, 1974, article in *The Oregonian* (published in Portland) reported that cutbacks in rail service, followed by Hughes Airwest having reduced the number of points it served, was causing a "crisis" in Oregon. (In 1995 and again in 1996, Amtrak further pared passenger train service in the state.)

More recently, the Associated Press reported that USAir Express, the sole airline serving Danville, Virginia, intended to stop flying to such point. Charlotte, the only city that this air carrier had served from Danville, could still be reached by Amtrak's Crescent. However, no longer having available to them the day trains once operated by the Southern

---

[37] Former section 13a of the Interstate Commerce Act, under which the ICC acted in discontinuance proceedings, was silent with respect to any mandatory resumption of services previously eliminated. Whether the agency possessed the power to require such resumption under this or any other statute is doubtful.

Railway between these cities, Crescent passengers arrive in Charlotte at 2:58 A.M. and in Danville at 4:15 A.M., times hardly compatible with civilized travel.

On February 19, 1995, the *Houston Chronicle* noted that American Airlines and/or Delta Air Lines had recently withdrawn from Lubbock and Midland-Odessa, Texas. Although smaller Southwest Airlines continued to serve these locations, in addition to such other Texas points as Amarillo and Corpus Christi that are reportedly in danger of losing their major air carriers, it is a difficult carrier for many connecting passengers to use. As an example, Southwest's main North Texas hub is situated at Love Field in Dallas, an airport served by no trunk airline. Moreover, Southwest refuses to handle interline checked baggage in cities where it does use common airports. (All of the Texas locations mentioned were once accorded first class rail service.)

C. Beneficiaries and Nonbeneficiaries of Air Carrier Deregulation

Congress began phasing out the regulatory power of the Civil Aeronautics Board in 1978. Some persons justify their endorsement of such a move on grounds that it both widened the carrier choice available to consumers (through unrestricted entry into the business) and resulted in a decline in the average air fare (through ensuing price competition). Such assertions are misleading in a variety of respects.

First, although a number of new carriers did initiate service, most of them lacked sustaining power and soon disappeared from the marketplace. Generally, those remaining are minor entities. Some function with what passengers have described as a "herd mentality." And while the traditional carriers have pursued acquisition of more routes, they have also exercised their newly acquired freedom to discontinue others.

Second, the new carriers typically equip their fleets with used airplanes which, although required to meet government safety standards, need excessive maintenance because of their old age. Hence, an inordinate number of flights are delayed or cancelled before takeoff. Moreover, older planes experience a higher rate of unscheduled landings arising from mechanical problems encountered aloft.

Third, when fare comparisons are used to evaluate deregulation, there is an implication that everything else has remained constant, *i.e.*, for particular origin-destination city pairs, nothing changed except that the fares were lower. What the low-fare proponents sometimes neglect to mention, however, is that deregulation also led to widespread implementation of the hub-and-spoke concept. Accordingly, passengers originating and terminating their journeys in smaller cities frequently no longer have direct flights available to them. Rather, they are now forced to go through an intermediate hub, a process resulting in the inconvenience of changing planes, more wear and tear on checked luggage, and an increase in total travel time. Therefore, unless a passenger travels solely between two hubs connected by a spoke, his postderegulation service typically has worsened.

Fourth, while the average fare likely has declined, the primary explanation therefor is that the industry has in recent years published a tier of low-level fares (with significant restrictions upon their use) to fill otherwise empty seats with passengers who previously either had traveled largely by bus and automobile or had seldom traveled at all. It is not clear that the airlines' traditional customers, whose generally inflexible travel itineraries usually preclude their qualifying for the low fares, have benefited greatly from fare deregulation.

But even those persons who can use reduced-fare tickets frequently encounter tariff provisions forcing them to spend Saturday night away from home, a requirement that may dissipate the supposed savings if it results in the addition of one or more extra nights' charges on their hotel bills while they wait around for Saturday to come and go.

Fifth, since the new carriers commonly pay low or no commissions to travel agents for issuing airplane tickets, travelers are learning that many agents are no longer willing to furnish certain ancillary services free of charge. These would include general travel advice; automobile rental and hotel reservations in connection with providers unwilling to grant commissions; and information on theatre performances, sporting events, etc. Hence, while some passengers are paying less for their tickets, they have begun paying for related trip amenities. Overall, they may have gained nothing.

Sixth, some smug people who brag about having obtained a cheap air fare later regret that they did not pay more. The circumstances usually arise when an airline needs to rebook passengers following travel disruptions caused by, for example, aircraft malfunction or severe weather. Unlike in predere gulation days—when carriers would attempt to equalize delay for all affected passengers by granting rebooking priority to those having been waiting the longest—now the carriers typically rebook higher-fare passengers first. Thus, passengers holding low-fare tickets on cancelled flights find themselves in limbo until seats can be located for all similarly stranded higher-fare passengers destined to the same point. If the airline operates a sufficient number of flights on the route in question, the penny-pinchers may be lucky enough to proceed with their journey the same day. But who knows?

D. Adverse Effects of Noise

With the unbridled entry into new markets and the concomitant expansion of existing ones, an exacerbation of noise problems has come to people on the ground. An article in *The Washington Post* for May 8, 1995, described the travails experienced by residents of Washington suburbs lying beneath runway approach paths. Accordingly, dozens of parents were complaining about an increase in air traffic waking and scaring babies. Other residents protested that persons talking on the street were being "drowned out."

Federal Aviation Administration (FAA) authorities charged with maintaining records of air traffic apparently are undercounting flights by treating first and second sections of New York shuttles as one airplane, rather than two. Commenting upon regulations requiring planes bound for National Airport to fly over water whenever possible, an FAA supervisor has acknowledged that jetliners "may be starting to turn the corner quicker." FAA's insistence upon making long-term studies of the validity of complaints was characterized by a resident as "an exercise in bureaucratic foot-dragging." Although late-night operations of loud jet aircraft are banned at National, no such restrictions apply at other local airports, *viz.*, Dulles and Baltimore-Washington.

Moreover, recent dedication speeches at the new Franklin D. Roosevelt memorial, planned as a place for solemn introspection on a Washington site reserved decades ago for a major historical display, were largely inaudible because of noise from planes landing at nearby National Airport. This is also close to a spot on the east bank of the Potomac River where summer concerts, once popular with boaters and seated patrons alike, cannot now be held because of incessant airplane noise.

A letter from a Jacksonville, Florida, woman to syndicated columnist Ann Landers (printed in newspapers on July 29, 1995) deplored the detrimental effect of larger aircraft then beginning to use that city's airport. Day and night, the woman bemoaned, she is now forced to insert ear plugs.

In an August 27, 1995, article published by *The Denver Post*, a long-time resident of Adams County, Colorado, was reported as complaining that blinding light beams from planes landing at the new Denver airport pierced her bedroom windows and that the accompanying noise rattled their frames. Additionally, an operator of a nearby farm declared that airplane noise had stopped her rabbits from breeding and caused her horses to injure themselves from "bolting from takeoff blasts that roll like thunder across the wheat and sunflower fields." Moreover, she said, "When the wind is right, you get an overwhelming smell of kerosene [that] can make you nauseous." Local homeowners say that the noise-complaint "hotline" is usually out of order.

These happenings at Denver, clearly diminishing the quality of life, were taking place in a city where Amtrak had already reduced rail service twice and later would do so a third time.

Finally, the journal *Environment and Behavior* revealed on page 638 of its September 1997 issue that Cornell University researchers have determined children attending school in the flight path of a major airport suffer reading comprehension deficits and speech perception impairments. These findings validate earlier studies by faculty members at New York University (published in 1981 in the *Journal of Personality and Social Psychology*, Volume 40, page 331) and at the University of Oregon and the University of California, Irvine (published in 1982 in the *Archives of Environmental Health*, Volume 37, page 24).

E. Weather-Induced Delays

People have known for some time that air travel is more susceptible than rail to disruption from adverse weather. This author is in possession of a news article from the now-defunct *Washington Star* describing the travails of George Washington University's basketball team. It seems that the players, attempting to return to Washington from an away game, were stranded at the Cincinnati airport because weather conditions prevented the plane from leaving.

In those days, the Chesapeake and Ohio Railway dispatched two evening departures on the Cincinnati-Washington route. After waiting all day and finally giving up on air service, the team decided to ride the second train (the Sportsman, departing shortly before midnight and arriving the middle of the following afternoon). If the players had not made the mistake of placing so much reliance on planes, they could have taken the early train—the George Washington—that arrived before 8:00 A.M. (Should the team become stranded in Cincinnati now, Amtrak would make it wait at that point until after 5:00 A.M. the following morning, or even longer if such day is other than Wednesday, Friday, or Sunday.)

The intent of this story is not to criticize everybody who desires to fly; certainly, the speed of airplanes can provide benefits enriching human life not otherwise attainable. Rather, the point is to demonstrate that air transportation is more vulnerable to the elements. That this vulnerability still haunts us was again vividly portrayed during the snowstorm that blanketed most of the Northeast on Sunday, January 7, 1996. Although Amtrak kept moving throughout, albeit with some delays and scattered cancellations, look what happened to air service.

On January 9, *The Boston Globe* reported that two big carriers operating in this area, American Airlines and USAir, together cancelled 1,500 flights over two days. According to *The Philadelphia Inquirer* (January 9), that municipality's airport remained completely closed until Monday evening; USAir, the dominant air carrier in the city, was unable to resume any flights there until Tuesday. On January 9, *The Sun*, published in Baltimore, related that a Maryland couple expecting to return by air from New

England found that only Amtrak could accommodate them. Although the train they rode arrived in Baltimore about on schedule, they then found themselves waiting for hours at the city's airport for their automobile to be liberated from the snowbound parking lot.

This newspaper also noted that at least seven hundred Trans World Airlines passengers destined for northeastern points were stranded in St. Louis. Interestingly, both the Baltimore and Ohio/Chesapeake and Ohio and Penn Central railroads operated direct St. Louis-East Coast trains (the George Washington and "Spirit of St. Louis," respectively) right up until Amtrak's start-up. This suggests that although both railroad systems had previously discontinued various other trains, the value to the public of these St. Louis runs overrode in importance any losses that such trains might have been incurring. Indeed, we learned in Chapter II, subchapter 5, that Amtrak's own St. Louis-Washington/New York National Limited had rebounded from early deficits to generate an operating profit in the very month it was first slated for discontinuance. It is likely that some of the aforementioned 700 stranded air passengers would have been ticketed on Amtrak if that carrier's 1996 schedules had not forced St. Louis-East Coast travelers into a circuitous detour through Chicago.

F. Matters of Safety

Responsibility for overseeing the safety of air commerce rests with the Federal Aviation Administration (FAA). Compared with other countries, the U.S. has achieved a low rate of airplane accidents. Nevertheless, it seems prudent to examine the system devised to protect air passengers from the inherent risks that they continue to face.

An article in *The Washington Post* for January 22, 1996, described the workings of the Automated Surface Observing System (ASOS) developed by the National Weather Service. The ASOS is an instrument cluster designed to perform many tasks traditionally accomplished by individuals. There were 126 of these units then commissioned and operating, mostly at airports, with a total of 247 planned by the end of the year. Unfortunately, the General Accounting Office had concluded that ASOS "does not provide certain capabilities...critical to ensuring safe aviation...."

For example, a unit installed at Richmond, Virginia, was registering precipitation simply as rain at times when the surface temperature hovered as low as twenty-one degrees. Local bulletins announcing the recorded rain conditions astonished city residents who could see obvious sleet merely by looking out their windows. The newspaper article further noted that for pilots and air traffic controllers, the difference between rain and sleet is "critical." Most of us laymen would likely agree. Yet, the Weather Service program manager responsible for ASOS did not think it should be abandoned because it was believed to function improperly "only in the most *extreme* weather conditions." [Emphasis added.] Readers can decide for themselves if January sleet in Richmond is an inconsequential extreme.

Another *Post* article on June 10, 1995, described three power outages—affecting air controllers' computers, radios, and radars—that occurred in FAA's New York facilities the previous spring. Although the agency insisted that safety was not compromised during these incidents, it traced the cause to "aging systems" not scheduled for replacement until 1998 and afterward. Meanwhile, repairmen knowledgeable about the older systems are fast retiring.

These outages came to the public's attention at the same time information was released concerning a fire aboard a taxiing ValuJet DC-9 at Atlanta that injured seven passengers and a flight attendant struck by exploding engine shrapnel. Probably not many ValuJet passengers were aware that all its planes, while cosmetically refurbished, were aged castoffs from other carriers (some foreign, and hence previously not subject to FAA maintenance inspection).

Additionally, rather than hire sufficient personnel of its own, this carrier—which now calls itself AirTran—typically used limited-term contracts to "farm out" key repair and other functions to a large number of multiple-customer service firms. Many of these entities commonly employed subcontractors, some of whom were not made aware of related work previously performed by others. Crucial tasks were left to individuals with neither an abiding loyalty to any single airline nor a sense of discipline that comes from having a long-term stake in the success of an enterprise.

Beyond safety considerations, a 1996 police investigation revealed that eight employees of one of the airline's contractors working at Washington's Dulles airport had pilfered a large quantity of personal articles from passengers' baggage. Authorities recovered about $10,000 worth of items, some at pawnshops.

The people whom this carrier actually did hire were paid minimal wages, meaning that passenger services suffered from a high turnover of employees constantly seeking opportunities to better themselves elsewhere.

A year after the Atlanta fire, another of the company's DC-9s crashed near Miami, leaving the future of this low-budget carrier and others like it open to serious question. Indeed, the FAA has from time to time exercised its authority to force service suspensions of a number of them after discovering that they had been engaging in unacceptable practices.

On December 15, 1994, *The Wall Street Journal* discussed problems exacerbated by the abandonment of jet service to smaller cities. Commuter aircraft filling the void were seen as having special risks, *viz.*, less sophisticated de-icing equipment and limited ability to climb above bad weather. Moreover, findings in a recent National Transportation Safety Board survey show that 87 percent of commuter plane pilots have flown while fatigued. A former chairman of the agency was quoted as acknowledging that commuter planes "aren't as safe." In 1995, the FAA decided to raise some (but not all) commuter training and safety standards to the level already imposed upon large carriers.

Even while the enhanced scrutiny was being applied, however, air passengers suffered in other ways, according to the *Kansas City Star* of August 2, 1995. When the FAA abruptly "grounded" bankrupt MarkAir (another low-budget carrier), six unaccompanied young children already en route were hastily removed from one of its planes stopped at Kansas City. They were spirited away to a local foster home because other air carriers would not honor their tickets and nobody on the scene could think of any other solution. It is hoped the children's sojourn in the home did not last long.

But even the FAA's best efforts to eliminate hazards do not fully guard against incidents such as that occurring aboard a commercial jet traveling from Newark to Atlanta. A bomb hoax, reported while the plane was over North Carolina, led to eight passengers sustaining injuries during an emergency evacuation at Greensboro, according to the *Greensboro News & Record* of December 30, 1995. (No reports appeared in that day's newspaper suggesting anything other than a normal trip for Amtrak's Crescent, operating over the same route.)

G. Medical Considerations

A medical advice column appearing in the September 7, 1969, issue of *The Plain Dealer* (published in Cleveland) dealt with the prudence that pregnant women should exercise in formulating their travel plans. George C. Thosteson, M.D., noted therein that aside from obvious risks associated with premature labor, the "date of confinement" in normal pregnancies may be misestimated by up to two weeks. Dr. Thosteson noted that one airline he contacted requests a physician's statement for flying after the seventh month of pregnancy. Another leading obstetrician refuses permission to fly after the eighth month. Passenger profile studies conducted today would probably show that women currently constitute a larger segment of the flying public than when the column in question was written. Therefore, the matter likely now affects a broader segment of the population than before.

Another medical condition foreclosing air travel is ear infection. According to the *Atlanta Journal-Constitution* of June 29, 1997, a mother and two children were forced to cancel a planned Atlanta-Los Angeles air journey when the daughter suddenly contracted an ear ailment that precluded her from flying for at least four days. Recognizing that Amtrak could get them to their destination sooner than a postrecovery flight, they switched to rail. As things turned out, all three had a marvelous time, and they certainly sound like candidates for future train excursions.[38] Luckily, this family was traveling between two points where Amtrak still operates (as of now, at least). Many less fortunate people no longer have the rail option.

Some travelers, in good health when they board an airplane, may be less healthy when they get off. In 1996, the World Health Organization (WHO) released information indicating that in the preceding year 22,812 persons contracted tuberculosis in the U.S. and that the rate of infection is rising rapidly. According to WHO, this is a disease that "can spread in the close confines of airliners." Moreover, spacing between rows of seats is getting tighter on airplanes, a factor known to medical science as leading to potentially fatal blood clots in the legs of taller passengers. We ought to ask ourselves if persons needing to travel in markets lacking rail service should be compelled to assume these risks.

Finally, our government should give due regard to the welfare of those travelers susceptible to sudden onslaughts of physical trauma. Current national transportation priorities forcing many of these persons to use air service deprive them of ready access to the kinds of emergency medical care available only from ground-based personnel.

H. What Commercial Air Travelers Can Expect These Days

To better comprehend the status of air travel today, let us picture a person not dissuaded from flying, despite the pitfalls described in the preceding sections. Indeed, imagine that this individual is about to take a hypothetical plane journey. We will go along and observe what transpires.

So as not to "stack the deck" against our traveler, let us suppose that (1) the trip does not involve Denver, where fares have risen sharply following the opening of that city's new $4.9 billion airport; (2) the destination is not one of the places described where a major carrier has deserted the market in favor of a less reliable commuter airline; (3) temperatures are unlikely to fall below freezing, and thus dupe an automated weather station into thinking that sleet is really rain; and (4) the traveler

---

[38] In the mother's words, the "brand-new first-class cabin sparkled." Her "children, new to such pampering, adored" the juice and snacks delivered to their room. "Sam, six, knew half the train's passengers by name. Ellen, three, remembers every tree, shrub and flower...[as well as] cactus replacing Georgia pines." In the diner, they ate "surprisingly well." After encountering another mother with whom she "immediately clicked," the two families "drank sweet tea and ogled [the sights] near the New Orleans train station," where they paused en route. At destination, "we were...sad. Our adventure was over. My kids saw a good chunk of America, not from 30,000 feet but firsthand, as we rolled across the land, mile by mile." This author could not have said it better.

is not in an advanced stage of pregnancy, afflicted with ear infection, or believed subject to a tumultuous physical crisis. With this introduction, let the trip begin.

The first step is selecting a flight and purchasing a ticket. Downtown sales offices are more difficult to find now, as some "old-line" carriers have been replaced by small companies lacking city offices. If our traveler is fortunate enough to find such an office, he discovers that the once-traditional industry practice of showing fares in timetables has been abandoned, forcing most customers to consume large amounts of time waiting in a ticket window line—or in a telephone booth—seeking information. While those persons having access to the proper computer equipment may be able to procure selected tickets electronically, about the only other alternative is to patronize a commercial travel agent (although some of these recently began charging fees). In most cases, the purchaser must trust the seller for the accuracy of fare quotes, since it is seldom practical to verify the prices.[39] But we shall assume that our traveler somehow secures a ticket at the correct fare.

The next task is determining how he will get to the airport. *The Washington Post* of May 19, 1995, contained an account of an out-of-town gentleman completing his afternoon business in the Georgetown section of Washington and desiring to go next to Cleveland, using air service from National Airport located across the Potomac River in Virginia. Those familiar with the area are aware that, although heavy rail transit serves the airport, it tunnels past Georgetown without stopping. Since the transit bureaucracy long ago discontinued direct buses between the District of Columbia and the airport, the gentleman had the choice of (1) taking a bus that goes toward the nearest rail transit station [discharging him not at the station, but rather, two blocks away], and then walking the remainder of the way to the station; (2) riding three buses, *i.e.*, transferring twice; or (3) hailing a taxicab.

If that traveler were familiar with the city, had sufficient time for multiple transfers, and were not carrying heavy luggage, he might have chosen the first or second of the numbered alternatives. Since, however, the gentleman was not cognizant of the transit routes, he hailed a taxi. If the trip had been by train departing from Union Station, the taxi driver would likely have proceeded east on Q Street (north of the congested Dupont Circle area) and at some point cut over to Massachusetts Avenue

---

[39] No person learned in the law has ever been able to satisfactorily explain to this author how society can denounce "bait and switch" advertising practiced by—for example—retail stores, but apparently find no objection when commonplace air carrier fare actions border so closely on such a tactic. Fine print caveats, revealing that these carriers may be unwilling to actually sell tickets at advertised prices to all potential passengers seeking to purchase them, somehow fail to mitigate the passenger frustration arising from repeated rebuffs at the ticket counter. Even Amtrak is now caught up in this tactic.

which goes past the station near the Capitol in the heart of town. But since the trip was to the Virginia side of the river, the man's taxi got slowed in rush hour traffic trying to squeeze onto the bridges.

Happily for that particular traveler, he made his plane, but just barely. How many others do not? And how many local drivers are delayed in getting to their destinations by all the airport-bound taxicabs cluttering the bridges? (Remember, as was said earlier in connection with the discussion on highway transportation, Washingtonians are driving more frequently now, because there are fewer city buses than ever to take them to the rail transit line.)

Let us hope that the passenger we are accompanying does not get caught in another dilemma, *viz.*—as the *Post* indicated in a December 23, 1995, article—enhanced security arising from fear of terrorism has led airlines to urge "travelers to arrive early enough to make their way through stricter checkpoints." In the summer of 1996, the president of the United States announced that the elapsed time between flight check-in and actual takeoff promised to get even longer.

Should our traveler be carrying a wrapped gift, he will be told, as an official was quoted in the newspaper as saying, "If security can't see what's inside, you [must] unwrap it." Indeed, a subsequent account reported that a woman en route to a wedding watched helplessly while an inspector tore away (ruined) a $5 customized paper wrapping, beautifully crafted by a department store expert, on a present intended for the newlyweds. Even if the inspector had not unwrapped the item, we can wonder how many dirty fingerprints he would have left on the paper, since the inspectors neither wash their hands nor don clean gloves between passengers. Of course, since this woman was traveling from Washington to New York, one of the few markets in which Amtrak currently exerts a serious effort to provide a realistic travel alternative, perhaps we should temper our sympathy.

Before leaving the subject of security, let us turn to another *Post* story, published January 14, 1996, about a different gentleman attempting to board a flight at another airport. He carried a money belt containing important documents, tickets, and $2,500 in cash and traveler's checks. At the metal detector, he was ordered to remove it. In the process of being "frisked," he lost sight of the belt; by the time he was released, it had disappeared. After about five minutes, a woman whose skycap had picked up the belt inadvertently with her belongings, returned and reunited the traveler with his property. A lucky outcome (albeit after a period of severe anxiety) in a dilemma that is, of course, never confronted by train passengers.

Returning to the sequential steps in our hypothetical traveler's flight, let us talk about some of the realities faced by present day air passengers, as compared with their parents' experiences in the early days of the jet age. Assuming that a traveler today actually boards the airplane (*i.e.*, the carrier has not "overbooked" and assigned the seat to someone else), he may find conditions observably less pleasant than in yesteryear: Seats are smaller, the angle of seat back recline has been reduced, spacing between rows is tighter, the ratio of passengers to both toilets and cabin attendants is higher, the proportion of fresh air in the cabin is lower, and food service is diminishing (if not gone).

But assume that our traveler acclimates himself to all the assorted vagaries and eventually reaches his destination airport. Then, unlike his train-riding counterpart who is met upon arrival by a redcap available to take his suitcases immediately to the taxicab-loading zone, the flyer must first wait in the airport baggage area, along with perhaps a hundred or more like individuals arriving at the same time, to retrieve his luggage that the air carrier required be checked. With a bit of luck, it is not damaged and no film has been streaked or fogged by powerful bomb-detecting x-ray machines now coming online, a concern recently validated by the Photographic and Imaging Manufacturers Association.

If our traveler's destination is downtown Boston, he may have to endure a ride from the airport similar to one taken not long ago by former Red Sox player Ted Williams. According to *The Boston Globe* of December 5, 1995, the legendary baseball star was caught in a 1 3/4-hour traffic jam, part of a continuing problem at least until 2004 when local authorities hope that a construction expenditure of up to $9.6 billion may have ameliorated some of the road bottlenecks. By contrast, Amtrak's Back Bay and South stations are conveniently located within the downtown Boston area, and the Route 128 and Framingham stations are situated to serve suburban points.

To be sure, countless air journeys are made daily with every aspect thereof unfolding as smoothly for the travelers as can be anticipated. For a particular air passenger to encounter all of the adverse happenings described above would be an anomaly. The point, however, is that the air mode most certainly is not clearly superior to rail in all its facets.

If one could correctly contend that revenues and taxes exacted from air passengers and other beneficiaries of the airways fully reimburse the carriers and the government for all economic costs expended in furnishing air transportation, the wisdom of Amtrak subsidies might be a fair subject for debate. We have seen, however, that the air trust fund falls considerably short in this regard. And with the losses or anemic profits characteristic of the airline industry in the recent past, federal income tax receipts from such entities have been minuscule.

Chapter IV
Amtrak's Critics:
Are Their Arguments Valid?

This chapter comprises discussions of three economic studies, miscellaneous remarks by United States senators, and a sampling of newspaper op-ed articles.

1. Amtrak Yesterday, Today and Tomorrow (Continental Trailways, Inc., 1976)

Continental Trailways, Inc. (CTI), acting on behalf of the 450 members of the National Association of Motor Bus Owners, prepared what it termed a "monograph" addressing criteria adopted by Amtrak's board of directors in complying with provisions of the Amtrak Improvement Act of 1975 calling for the formalization of corporate policy guidelines. These criteria embraced economic, social, and environmental implications arising from the operation of a national rail passenger system. The monograph contained background material presented to Congress in support of CTI's proposal that restraints be imposed upon Amtrak's federal appropriations.

    A. Level of Amtrak Subsidy

CTI declared that implicit in Amtrak's criteria was an overriding determination to maintain and expand its service "at any price." According to CTI, Amtrak's "[s]ubsidy should be phased down over a period of years [and should in no case] be greater than 50% of its operating costs.... [It] is inequitable for the taxpayer to contribute larger sums to Amtrak's support than does the user of its service." CTI further alleged that "Amtrak's traffic is subsidized at a rate almost ten times that of the subsidized airline industry."

In addressing CTI's "at any price" charge, we should note that under initial legislation creating the network, the secretary of transportation identified the "end points" between which mandatory service would be provided; Amtrak's board had no control over the designation of such points. Additionally, establishment later of "experimental routes" arose out of a direct congressional mandate. Moreover, a significant part of the post-1971 expansion of the system came at the behest of certain states desirous of starting particular services. Therefore, the "at any price" accusation directed against Amtrak's board does not appear well placed.

Relative to CTI's proposed 50 percent ceiling above which no subsidy would be paid, we should note that Amtrak's coverage of its operating expenses has been generally improving. For example, the company's 1992 annual report showed on the inside front cover that by 1988 the revenue-to-expense ratio had reached .69 and that it had continued to climb so that it was at .79 in 1992.

CTI's reference to Amtrak's subsidy being at a level nearly ten times that of airlines is supported solely by a vague reference to unspecified data compiled by the Civil Aeronautics Board. Probably the air subsidy to which it refers consists only of direct payments to specific carriers, thereby excluding costs underwritten by government in furnishing the airway and the airport facilities used by all the airlines. The latter costs are substantial. (See Chapter III, subchapter 2.)

B. Cohesiveness of Rail Network

CTI claimed that Amtrak's route network appeared not to have fostered the "integrated national rail passenger system" called for in its congressional mandate and that there was an absence of desired "synergism." Additionally, CTI contended that even the most heavily patronized trains are inefficient, since they can have route circuity up to 45 percent.

On these charges, CTI is largely accurate (although the problems are correctable). In Chapter VII, we will discuss the subject in depth.

C. Effect of Length of Rail Haul upon Losses

In a section of its monograph discussing the geographical distribution of losses, CTI asserted that in terms of 1975 fully allocated losses per passenger-mile as taken from Amtrak records, the short-haul routes were generally poorer performers than their longer-distance counterparts.

However, this author's examination of records covering the short-haul trains then experiencing troubling losses reveals that the issue has since largely vanished. That is to say, most of these trains either were subsequently discontinued (*e.g.*, Chicago-Dubuque, Philadelphia-Harrisburg in part, and Washington-Cumberland) or have gained improved ridership through intensive marketing programs undertaken by particular states (California, Illinois, Michigan, Washington, *etc.*).

As noted in the preface, it is not the intent of this volume to delve into the economics of locally supported regional services. However, in response to CTI, it should be recognized that many studies of Amtrak's financial situation (including those most prejudicial to the carrier) have concluded that despite possible high investment and maintenance costs, selected short-haul services possess a more favorable economic potential than long-haul trains equipped with such expensive amenities as sleeping cars.

D. Intermodal Competition

CTI disputed Amtrak's belief that despite some people's negative attitude toward passenger trains, the public would welcome the prospect of improved rail service. According to CTI, technological developments benefiting the highway and air modes—along with the "intangible quality of togetherness" achieved in an automobile—preclude a resurgence in rail travel. Moreover, CTI stated that *vis-a-vis* air service for which trip duration time may be less, trains "cannot be maintained at comparable levels of cleanliness." Additionally, the "metal-on-metal contact of rail vehicles aggravates the malfunction rate of heating and air conditioning devices...[and] vibration intrinsic to the movement of train on track creates additional discomfort...."

With regard to improvements in highway and airway travel, no reasonable person would suggest Amtrak has denied that such modes merit a place in the overall transportation market or that passenger rail can provide all the intercity travel needs of a modern society. On the other hand, documentation in the preceding chapter of the shortcomings of these competitive modes suggests that Amtrak's freedom from such burdens can be a positive factor in marketing rail travel.

Relative to the effect of length of haul upon cleanliness, this author has observed both dirty, short-haul trains and clean, long-haul trains. Solving any problems in this regard seems more a matter of better crew supervision than something intrinsic in length of haul.

Lacking any proffered explanation as to why "metal-on-metal" (wheel/rail contact) might be more deleterious than the "rubber-on-asphalt" inherent in buses rolling on a highway or airplanes landing on a runway, CTI's view seems speculative at best, and therefore, unpersuasive.

As to relative discomfort from vehicular motion, the public has never demanded the placement of airplane-style "sickness bags" on trains, suggesting that such an alleged shortcoming of rail is imaginary.

E. Amtrak Fare Level

According to CTI, Amtrak pursues a "schizophrenic" pricing policy that on the one hand generates revenues inadequate to recoup its expenses, and on the other, causes economic injury to buses by undercutting their fares. CTI claims that bus carriers have been forced to reduce fares to the level of rail in a number of markets. It singles out a particular bus route as having especially suffered, *viz.*, Chicago-Flint, where Indian Trails, Inc., reputedly was forced to lay off employees after Amtrak reintroduced rail service in 1974.

We should, however, take note of CTI's failure to mention that the Flint train in question here (the Blue Water) was inaugurated with financial support provided by the state of Michigan.[40] This train proved so popular with Michigan residents that the state later extended its support to other trains as well. The fact that, as far as we know, Michigan has not subsidized Indian Trails on this route suggests its citizens prefer trains to buses.

2. Amtrak: An Experiment in Rail Service (Frank P. Mulvey, 1978)

Frank P. Mulvey, a professor at Northeastern University, prepared the captioned paper at the request of the National Transportation Policy Study Commission. This author has abstracted the salient points therein because they mirror a number of arguments frequently raised by those seeking to justify dismantling the country's rail passenger network.

A. Safety

Professor Mulvey undertook to determine the number of lives that Amtrak saves yearly by providing a travel alternative to persons who would otherwise be forced to use automobiles. He developed a mathematical formula incorporating certain assumptions, *i.e.*, (1) half of all passengers riding long-distance trains make short trips, (2) 5 percent of all short-distance train passengers [outside the Northeast Corridor] make long trips, (3) 75 percent of the short-distance passengers would otherwise use automobiles, and (4) 25 percent of the long-distance passengers also would exercise this option. Using a 1971-73 fatality rate of 1.4 deaths per 100 million automobile passenger-miles (derived from a

---

[40] Actually, the Blue Water operated to Port Huron. Later, it was renamed the International and extended to Toronto.

figure of 1.8 deaths published by the National Association of Motor Bus Owners, adjusted downward to eliminate pedestrian and bicycle accidents), the formula estimated that thirty-three lives were saved.

Based upon U.S. Department of Transportation studies indicating that the expected lifetime earnings of victims average $300,000 per fatality—or $1 million when adjusted for loss of services to family, friends, and community—Amtrak's annual contribution is likely worth about $33 million. In addition, Professor Mulvey calculated that the existence of Amtrak enables the nation to avoid an estimated $18 million in societal costs arising from nonfatal accidents.

After thus setting forth the claimed value of the passenger carrier in terms of safety (amounts predicated, of course, upon the traffic base generated on its minuscule system), Professor Mulvey suggested, "Monies devoted to Amtrak could be dedicated toward improving highway safety or the crash-worthiness of automobiles. These programs might generate a much greater return per dollar spent than results from supplying rail services."

Doubtless, most informed Americans are aware that public and private agencies have expended considerable effort over the years in developing a safer highway infrastructure. Statistical studies show that the interstate system, presumably the road choice of most rail passengers ousted from their trains were Amtrak to terminate its long-distance operations, has a better safety record than older highways. Since, however, the interstates have for the most part been in place for a generation, it would be expected that pending the introduction of futuristic systems such as electronic guideways, etc., we will be seeing diminishing returns from further efforts to improve safety.

Also, it seems doubtful that train passengers would be willing to sacrifice the safest form of surface travel for the highway simply because research on "crash-worthy" automobiles may succeed some day in reducing the severity of the road accidents to which they would be subjected. Mild accidents may be preferable to bad accidents, but not to no accidents.

B. Energy

Using per passenger-mile energy costs expressed on a British thermal unit basis for the various transport modes, Professor Mulvey calculated that operation of Amtrak trains saves the nation 53 million gallons of fuel annually. He equated this quantity to $29.2 million in avoided costs.

However, he also said, "Bus outperforms rail in every market. If traffic currently diverted to Amtrak had been diverted to bus, the savings would be much larger." He further stated, "There may be more cost-effective ways to [conserve energy] such as 100 percent compliance with the 55 m.p.h. speed limit...."

In the preceding chapter, we saw that in the years following 1971 when bus carrier management was presented with a marvelous opportunity to gain ridership following the discontinuance of so many trains not incorporated into Amtrak, buses were unable to attract and retain the previous rail passengers. In its 1977 report to Congress on the effectiveness of the 1970 Amtrak act, the Interstate Commerce Commission stated on page 37, "Rail transportation competes to a limited degree with bus carriers, confined almost solely to riders traveling short distances within densely populated centers. *Few people take long bus rides.*" [Emphasis added.] Also, as we saw in subchapter 1, the people of Michigan largely did not want intercity buses; rather, they desired passenger rail. There is no reason to believe that residents of other states hold a different view.

Moreover, the dominant bus carrier—Greyhound—has scaled back its long-haul service. Traditionally, that firm included a full page of schedules in *Russell's Official National Motor Coach Guide* showing, for example, multiple East Coast-Los Angeles runs, with a single change of bus at Memphis. By the 1990s, no such schedules appeared. Persons then attempting to ascertain the particulars of transcontinental bus travel were required to piece together departure and arrival times from separate tables in the guide. This author's experience has been that it is virtually impossible these days to obtain printed schedule leaflets from Greyhound. In short, long-haul bus service is seldom a reasonable alternative.

Finally, although adherence to the 55 m.p.h. maximum speed limit may have seemed a desirable course for achieving energy conservation in 1978, when Professor Mulvey speculated that doing so might be more productive than enhancing rail travel, it no longer is. Obviously, in light of the official abandonment of such limit in 1995, this asserted reason for discouraging Amtrak patronage has been proven to lack long-term validity.

C. Environment

Professor Mulvey identified several categories of transport vehicle emissions contributing to air pollution. Table 3 shows the effect that long-distance rail passenger service has upon each. Note that for the first category shown, there is a net reduction; for the next four, a net increase.[41]

---

[41] So that readers might gauge the validity of these figures, this author has obtained analogous data covering three of the pollutants. Such data were assembled by the staff of the Interstate Commerce Commission in Finance Docket No. 28697, *Southern Railway Company, Discontinuance of Train Nos. 1 and 2, the Southern Crescent, between Washington, D.C. and New Orleans, Louisiana.* The data indicated that if this train service had not operated and all passengers had used automobiles instead, for the year there would have been an increase in carbon monoxide emissions of 575.5 tons and reductions in hydrocarbon and nitrogen oxide emissions of 5.6 and 400.9 tons, respectively.

Table 3
Effect of Train Service upon Pollution Abatement

Type of Pollutant	Tons Reduction per Year
(1) Carbon monoxide or CO	4,868
(2) Hydrocarbons or HC	(373)
(3) Nitrogen oxides or No_x	(5,622)
(4) Sulphur oxides or So_x	(756)
(5) Particulates	(259)

Although acknowledging the reduction in carbon monoxide achievable through the use of rail service, Professor Mulvey stated that since this kind of pollution "is primarily an urban phenomenon and long-distance trains spend relatively little time passing through urban areas...[it] argues for restructuring the Amtrak route network to concentrate on short-distance markets where environmental effects of reducing auto travel may be meaningful." Even here, however, he contended that if California standards governing vehicular emission of hydrocarbons and nitrogen oxides were implemented generally, motor vehicles could achieve roughly the same reduced level of emissions that Amtrak realizes on its short-distance and Metroliner services.[42]

The response to this charge is simply that while pollution abatement is frequently cited as a desirable goal of mass transportation, it was included neither in the "Declaration of Purpose" enacted by Congress for Amtrak (Section 101 of the Rail Passenger Services Act) nor in the criteria used by the secretary of transportation in designing Amtrak's network. (See Chapter II, subchapter 1.) Air quality improvements derived through diversion of persons from automobiles to trains are ancillary benefits only, and therefore, not controlling with respect to deciding where Amtrak should target its marketing.

D. Summary

In concluding his paper, Professor Mulvey made certain sweeping pronouncements: "The number of Amtrak routes could be reduced and train services on the remaining routes...provided at less frequent intervals, lowering the expense of operating Amtrak. For the services that remain...those who choose to use passenger trains should pay the cost of the resources they consume." "It may be...in other corridors [than the Northeast]...that Amtrak could shift equipment to such markets to provide more frequent service." "Sleepers and dining cars might not be

---

[42] Since Professor Mulvey's study, the introduction of diesel locomotives equipped with microprocessor-activated fuel injection systems has diminished emission of nitrogen oxides. For further discussion of this subject, see *Passenger Train Journal*, March 1996, page 31.

usable at all, and other cars might have to be reconfigured to allow for higher seating densities."[43]

The patience of readers is requested until Chapters VI, VII, VIII, and IX where we will deal at length with the subject matters alluded to in the above mélange of plaints. The discussions therein should help dispose of these criticisms.

3. Amtrak: The National Railroad Passenger Corp. (George W. Hilton, 1980)

Distributed by the American Enterprise Institute for Public Policy Research (Washington, D.C.), this paper identifies the author as a professor of economics at the University of California, Los Angeles, and an adjunct scholar of the institute. After reciting a brief history of rail passenger service, much of which was covered in Chapters I and II of this volume, he undertook a detailed examination of certain aspects of Amtrak's operation and its outlook. So that readers may anticipate what lies ahead here, this author will quote at the outset Professor Hilton's basic conclusion: "The Amtrak experiment has been unsuccessful by any standard."

A. Demand Conditions

In a discussion comparing alternative modes of travel, Professor Hilton referred to a general survey (released by the Department of Transportation in January 1978) that polled Amtrak passengers as to how they would have reacted if the train they were riding had not operated. The replies disclosed that 48 percent would otherwise have traveled in automobiles, 23 percent on buses, and 22 percent on planes. (The remainder did not respond.)

In the West, where discretionary travel is believed more prevalent, a University of Idaho survey conducted in April-June of that year revealed that only 12 percent of Amtrak passengers would have selected bus as an alternative.[44] An additional 24 percent would not have traveled at all, including a disproportionately high number of railroad employees riding on passes.

Commenting on these surveys, Professor Hilton said the fact that so few Amtrak passengers would have considered going by bus may be

---

[43] This author recalls that when the Pennsylvania Railroad once increased seating capacity in a series of coaches, such cars emerged from the shop with some pairs of seats having no adjacent windows. Surely, Amtrak would not wish to make the same mistake.

[44] Professor Hilton speculated that the failure of more western rail travelers to specify a switch to bus may be explained by a second Seattle train then available west of Minneapolis, and by the sparseness of bus service in areas served by the Empire Builder on its routing predominately via the former Great Northern Railway.

surprising because, based upon 1976 surveys of Amtrak and Greyhound riderships undertaken by the respective managements, he found the demographic characteristics of train and bus passengers "quite similar." However, he suggested that although there exists a pool of people indifferent as to whether they travel by rail or by bus, Amtrak does not attract many of these because the comparative infrequency of train departures on long-distance routes deters their considering that mode. Let us now examine these assertions.

The Amtrak and Greyhound surveys of train and bus passengers categorized various passenger attributes: sex, education, age, household income, and trip purpose. While some of these attributes were not widely dissimilar for the two modes, it appears that others were. For example, consider the two categories depicted in Table 4:

Table 4
Comparative Passenger Demographics

	Train	Bus
Education		
Grade school or less	4.6%	9.0%
High school	38.6%	35.0%
Household Income (annual)		
Under $5,000	15.6%	18.0%
$5,000-$14,999	36.1	47.0
$15,000 and over	40.2	20.0
Not reported	....	15.0

Under the education category, we can see that for grade school or less, the bus component is almost twice that of train. Strangely, no percentages are provided for college-educated passengers; nevertheless, data for the latter are available elsewhere. Thus, the 1972 *Census of Transportation* (U.S. Government, Bureau of the Census) indicated that 50.1 percent of train passengers were college-educated, while only 24.3 percent of the bus passengers were. In other words, college-educated passengers traveled on trains at a rate more than twice that of buses. Considering the wide variation in these key education components, it is doubtful that Professor Hilton should have concluded that train and bus passenger demographics are "quite similar."

For the household income category, the Bureau of Economics division of the Interstate Commerce Commission (ICC), analyzing the same 1972 census data, noted on page 29 of its 1978 study titled *The Intercity Bus Industry* that, "A majority of intercity bus travelers have relatively low household incomes [whereas] middle income travelers...appear predominant for intercity rail travel." Again, full analysis reveals that train and bus passengers are not at all as similar as Professor Hilton would have us believe.

The interpretation to be made of all this is that Professor Hilton may be correct in his assertion that persons for whom frequent departures are critical are less likely to ride trains in the first place. But for people who do, careful analysis confirms that their demographic profile does not resemble that of typical bus passengers. Unless unavoidably forced to switch to buses, not many rail riders would do so because (according to the ICC, as stated in subchapter 2) other than a residual hard core, most people dislike long bus rides. And, as the surveys discussed above suggest, middle-income and college-educated persons (*i.e.*, the people more inclined to ride trains) use buses to a significantly less extent.[45]

B. Cost Conditions

Professor Hilton discovered a 1978 General Accounting Office (GAO) report which he used to buttress his hypothesis that "Amtrak will probably suffer a...long atrophy and finally be discontinued." The report, titled *Should Amtrak Develop High-Speed Corridor Service Outside the Northeast?* (CED-78-67), included an economic analysis of the westbound Twilight Limited, operating in the late afternoon/early evening from Detroit to Chicago.

From his reading of the GAO report, Professor Hilton claimed that "Amtrak allocated expenses of $143,898 to the train for the month of June 1977...." If this entire amount were to have been recovered from passenger revenue, the average fare would have to have been $29.80 rather than the price then charged of $20.50. Although Professor Hilton omitted from his book some of the data needed for us to comprehend Amtrak's accounting procedure, the requisite details appeared in the GAO report, a copy of which is in the possession of this author.

To keep the record straight, the entire $143,898 was not "allocated" as Professor Hilton asserts. Rather, as GAO stated on page 19 of its report, the Twilight Limited "incurred *or* was allocated expenses totaling $143,898." [Emphasis added.] There is a significant difference between incurred and allocated expenses. The former type of expense (an example of which is crew wages) is a direct one traceable to a particular train. The latter type (track maintenance, for example) is usually incurred for the benefit of multiple trains and can be allocated to a particular train only on

---

[45] There is no explanation in Professor Hilton's book for an apparent inconsistency in data supporting the average Amtrak trip length. On page 35, he refers to 1978 hearings before the House of Representatives (dealing with 1979 appropriations) wherein the average 1977 trip was stated to have been 270 miles. However, 4.3 billion passenger-miles in 1977 (page 33) divided by 19.2 million passengers for that year (page 49) equals 224 miles.

some arbitrary basis using various measures of relative use. We will refer to this type of expense as "nondirect."

To understand the composition of the Twilight Limited's expenses, we must examine GAO's page 11 for an expense separation between "direct," "common," "operating support," "depreciation, taxes, and insurance," and "other." Since, as we said above, only the direct expenses are incurred by—and hence, are traceable to—particular trains, it is highly relevant to learn how much of the $143,898 monthly amount is classified as "direct." Because none of the nondirect expenses allocated to the Twilight Limited would have been avoided if the train had not operated, Amtrak was better off by running it as long as the revenue exceeded the direct expenses.

According to GAO, for the study month the Twilight Limited incurred direct expenses in three categories. Expressed on a per day basis, these were $893-labor, $195-fuel, and $127-other expenses. GAO also determined that such direct expenses could have been completely recouped through carrying an average of 102 passengers per trip. Since for the study month the Twilight Limited enjoyed an average passenger count of 161, we can readily see that the revenue more than covered the direct expenses.

For Amtrak to be made whole, of course, its collective income from revenues and subsidies must at least equal its collective expenses, *i.e.*, both (1) the direct expenses incurred by particular trains; and (2) the nondirect expenses arising from simply being in business and that, unless there is a drastic change in the size of the system, do not fluctuate with the number of trains operated.

In theory, to the extent that passenger revenues accruing to any particular train are insufficient to cover all its arbitrarily allocated nondirect expenses, other trains must absorb the deficiency. Unfortunately, most recent studies of U.S. intercity passenger train economics have shown that no Amtrak train enjoys revenues ample enough to defray all of its own arbitrarily allocated nondirect expenses, let alone provide a cushion by which to absorb such expenses for other trains. The conventional deficit-reduction approach of the Department of Transportation and some others has been to discontinue selected trains, with the expectation that a substantial portion of their passengers would be accommodated on surviving trains. As we saw in Chapter II, subchapter 6, this tactic failed miserably in 1979, because the predicted diversion largely did not materialize.

Many of Amtrak's critics say that ridership may have peaked, and since the carrier sustains significant losses per passenger handled, the entire enterprise should be put up for sale (at scrap value, if need be). There is another solution. In the situation before us, the revenue accruing to the westbound Twilight Limited was depressed because despite its value to local passengers, the time of day in which it operated precluded (1) any other train from feeding it passengers at Detroit, and (2) any other train from receiving its passengers at Chicago. Stated differently, there was—and still remains—a problem of lack of connections. In Chapters VII and VIII, we shall discuss the connectivity question further.

Before leaving Professor Hilton, however, there are a few more matters to contemplate. While the direct expenses incurred by the Twilight Limited constituted 25.3 percent of its total expenses, one "catch-all" subcategory of the common expenses that Amtrak allocated to the train (*i.e.*, reservation, marketing, ticketing, pensions, etc.) made up 30.1 percent of the total. In this author's judgment, it was poor accounting practice to have grouped such dissimilar common items together when doing so created a sum larger than the total direct expenses.

But another question arises here, *viz.*, was it logical for the grouped items to have loomed so large? In Amtrak's annual report for a recent year (1994), "train operations" and "marketing and reservations" constituted 21.3 percent and 7.8 percent, respectively, of "total expenses." (Pensions, also grouped in the catch-all figure charged to the Twilight Limited, are not shown separately in the 1994 annual report.) The inverse relationship between direct expenses and the catch-all expenses in the GAO report appears peculiar.[46]

4. United States Senators (1985)

There follow selected remarks concerning a budget resolution that were made May 9, 1985, on the floor of the U.S. Senate (Ninety-ninth Congress, First Session). Readers are invited to draw their own conclusions relative to the appropriateness of the senators' observations.

"One would think Congress could recognize a turkey when it saw one, but as incredible as it may seem, Congress continues to use the taxpayers' money to operate Amtrak."

He quoted an unnamed observer as having said, "Amtrak is not providing a system of transportation but a form of kinetic art."
Sen. William L. Armstrong, Colorado

"Amtrak carries one-quarter of one percent of...people who travel between cities.... It is not essential to our national transportation picture, or to the Northeast Corridor."
Sen. John C. Danforth, Missouri

---

[46] In a February 17, 1978, letter to the GAO, Amtrak President Paul H. Reistrup complained that the report at issue here "misses a number of points," "fails to comprehend important activity underway," "fails to properly depict the effect of inflation," is "weak and incomplete," and "fails to place preliminary studies...in context."

"...virtually the same day Amtrak went thundering out of the prairies of Wyoming, for what is considered a more picturesque view of the Colorado Rocky Mountains, I successfully authored an amendment to the fiscal year 1984 Department of Transportation appropriations bill reducing Amtrak's subsidy by $1.6 million—or the amount the President of Amtrak claimed the Corporation would save by terminating its service to my State...When Amtrak abandoned Wyoming almost 2 years ago, it left the State without any passenger train service for the first time in about 100 years. Yet, Wyoming taxpayers have been forced to maintain Amtrak service to other parts of the country for several years now, and I believe that's far too long...."[47]

Sen. Malcolm Wallop, Wyoming

It should be pointed out that other senators adopted a more favorable position toward Amtrak, as the following passages show:

Sen. Joseph R. Biden (Delaware) noted, in connection with hopes of anti-Amtrak forces that other operators would step in if Amtrak were to exit the business, that "Privately owned rail passenger service is not going to reappear out of Amtrak's grave. Once we close the books on Amtrak, that's it, no more intercity travel by rail in this country. The obstacles to reestablishing national rail service would be too much for anyone to overcome.... [T]he Office of Management and Budget has painted a pretty picture of a nation barely noticing when Amtrak ceases to exist.... [I]t's fairy-tale stuff.[48]

Sen. Dave Durenberger (Minnesota) noted that "The Amtrak issue is not an issue of subsidies as much as it is an issue of a national commitment to a transportation system."

Sen. Arlen Spector (Pennsylvania) observed that if Amtrak were eliminated, "Traffic will be snarled all over the east coast, with highways jammed and airports clogged. It would become impossible for traffic to get through the Baltimore Harbor Tunnel. In fact, the U.S. Senate might have difficulty getting a quorum."

Sen. Alfonse M. D'Amato (New York) complained that the administration's proposed budget "would simply abandon Amtrak and throw

---

[47] Subsequently, Amtrak returned to Wyoming when the Pioneer was established on its Chicago-Denver-Portland-Seattle route. Now, of course, it is again gone from Wyoming.

[48] Relative to the difficulty which private operators might face in taking over Amtrak routes, an article in *Railway Age* for July 1995 noted on page 12 that without the full faith and credit of the U.S. that currently backs Amtrak, the freight railroads would be wary of entering into new operating agreements.

away the billions of dollars of Federal investment in the passenger railroad's infrastructure and rolling stock."

5. Miscellaneous Newspaper "Op-Ed" Articles (1985-95)

This author has encountered assorted articles having a theme similar to those in subchapters 1 through 4, *viz.*, dismantle Amtrak. Regrettably, some of them deal quite facetiously with this very serious topic. Few pretend to approach the subject with scholarly bent. One is so vile, sickening, and disgusting that it falls into a category normally rejected by reputable newspapers. None deserves comment, but snippets are presented here so readers may see the kind of mentality that Amtrak faces in some quarters.

"[M]emories of a simpler age...[have] no place in the federal budget. In an age of fiscal austerity, the traditional charity toward Amtrak is as obsolete as a steam locomotive."

Chicago Tribune, February 24, 1985

* * * * *

"Amtrak is essentially a government subsidy for people who are afraid to fly, and retired people who have the time to spend a month crawling across North Dakota....

"Two days into a trip, and you start worrying about the effects of second-hand socks....

"[The then-recent elimination of service to a large number of stations and the discharge of 5,500 workers] will help, but there probably isn't a billion dollars [his rough estimate of the deficit] worth of savings in those actions. Not even if they vacuum up the loose change in the seats....

"Trains are romantic; they have that haunting whistle, those great chuffing engines: *LOO*singmoney, *LOO*singmoney, *LOO*singmoney....

"[Amtrak is] like the state airline for an irrelevant socialist nation....

"The main difference between the dining car and a cattle shoot is that Amtrak doesn't end your visit with a nail gun....

"Try getting a train to stop so you can enjoy a scenic overlook. It can be done—there's a little red lever in every car....

"Trains killed the stagecoach. If the government then was like the one we have now, we'd still be debating the fate of Amhoof."

Cleveland Plain Dealer, December 25, 1994

* * * * *

"[A] more suitable name would be Don't Give a Damtrak...."

"Amtrak has become the boondocks equivalent of the big-city, big-league sports franchise: If you haven't got one, you're out of it...."

"[Even after the proposed discontinuances, Amtrak] will still be running decrepit trains on outmoded tracks...."

The Washington Post, April 10, 1995

* * * * *

"[F]or every 1,000 travelers who go from one city to another, only three take Amtrak. Unfortunately for American motorists, two are powerful U.S. senators...from Delaware."

The Denver Post, August 23, 1995

* * * * *

After referring to a certain American slang phrase ("Helluva way to run a railroad": "Speaking of Amtrak...."

Alluding to a lament once expressed by President Nixon [who signed the original Amtrak legislation] that he had had a childhood ambition to become a railroad engineer: "Would that he had."

At a time when the latest reductions in intercity rail service were making it increasingly difficult for travelers to secure train space: "Amtrak ads are not producing congestion down at the old railroad depot."

The Washington Post, October 8. 1995

* * * * *

"Government exists to advance national interests....[R]ailroad buffs...don't qualify."

The Washington Post, November 15, 1995

Chapter V
Amtrak's Missed Opportunities

Sometime back in the 1970s, the University of Maryland and the University of Minnesota football teams competed in a postseason bowl game at Birmingham, Alabama. Both Southern Railway's independently operated Southern Crescent and Amtrak's Floridian then served Birmingham. From Maryland's campus at College Park, it was an easy trip on a Baltimore and Ohio commuter train to Washington Union Station, the nearest point for boarding the Southern Crescent. Minnesota's campus was located a short distance from Amtrak's former Hennepin Avenue station in downtown Minneapolis, where one could board a train to Chicago and connect with the Floridian.

The game seemed a natural draw for students and alumni from both schools wishing to cheer their teams to victory. Yet if either Amtrak or Southern expended any special effort to attract football fans on their respective Birmingham trains, it escaped the attention of this author (both a Maryland graduate and a 1970s resident of Minneapolis) who would have welcomed some kind of railroad-sponsored group deal offering camaraderie as well as transportation.

When no word came of any special arrangements, the thought presented itself that lackadaisical marketing may pose problems for these trains' long-term viability. Sure enough, Amtrak subsequently discontinued the Floridian, and Southern applied to discontinue the Crescent.[49] Was there a missed opportunity here?

The above-described situation raises the question as to whether a transportation firm viewed by the law as a common carrier has any public obligation to stimulate traffic over its system. Basic economics holds that industries such as railroads, characterized by labor intensity and heavy investment in plant and equipment, need ample revenues from which to recover the associated high level of fixed costs. Therefore, would it be presumptuous of us to expect that passenger railroads would

---

[49] The eventual solution devised for the problems of the independently operated Southern Crescent was to incorporate it into Amtrak's system.

maximize ticket sales by soliciting additional customers to augment the patronage of those loyal travelers who can be taken for granted to simply show up at the depot at train time?

In pre-Amtrak days, airlines commonly provided copies of their timetables for hotel lobby brochure racks; railroads were not always as diligent.[50] Although a few individual railroads and The Pullman Company once advertised in newspapers and magazines, Amtrak seems to do a better job (including television commercials). It promotes service to a number of popular destinations, some of which are served at a desirable time of day. Commonly, however, Amtrak's sparse schedules fall short of satisfying the potential market. There follow some examples. (Train times shown below were those published for fall/winter, 1995-96.)

One of this country's eminent traditions is the annual running of the Kentucky Derby at Churchill Downs in Louisville, Kentucky. Probably the best known event in horse racing, it attracts spectators from far and wide. Just before Amtrak's start-up, Louisville was served by three passenger trains: a branch of the George Washington (connecting the city with the Northeast), the Pan-American (on its Cincinnati-New Orleans run), and the South Wind (one of two Chicago-Florida trains). Amtrak retained Chicago-Florida service over this route for a while. But now, the Derby city—metropolis of Kentucky and busy commercial, educational, and manufacturing center—has no rail passenger service. A missed opportunity.

In late 1995, the Rock and Roll Hall of Fame and Museum opened in Cleveland, Ohio. Owing to the wide popularity of the music honored, the media has accorded this attraction national attention. Undoubtedly, the city expected the facility to generate substantial tourist income. Considering the acclaimed architectural attributes of the structure and its placement a few blocks from the new baseball park and future rebuilt football stadium, as well as maritime exhibits and pleasure boat cruises centered on the Lake Erie shoreline, the city's expectations probably were not unrealistic.

So how well does Amtrak serve Cleveland? If rock-and-roll fans are coming from New York City or Boston, the answer is that they can get there fairly easily on the overnight Lake Shore Limited. But when they wish to return home, they must depart in the middle of the night at 3:46 A.M. Similarly, fans coming from Chicago cannot get to Cleveland before the Capitol Limited's 2:04 A.M. arrival. Returning, they either stay awake until the Capitol Limited's 3:17 A.M. departure or arise at a predawn hour to make the 6:36 A.M. Lake Shore Limited. Fans from Cincinnati or Amtrak-served points in the central South must travel circuitously via either

---

[50] As a convenience to their guests, some hotels (the former Statler Hilton in Detroit comes to mind) once posted on the wall near the bell captain's desk a directory of principal passenger train departures. This author is unaware of any U.S. hotel currently maintaining such a practice.

Washington or Chicago. With these schedules, not many rock-and-roll fans are likely to travel to Cleveland on Amtrak. Another missed opportunity.

A further example of a new popular attraction is the Mall of America, located in Bloomington, Minnesota (a southern suburb of Minneapolis-St. Paul, the fifteenth largest U.S. urban area). An article in *The Washington Post* for June 4, 1995, described this shopping mecca as "the third most popular tourist attraction in the United States, after Disney World in Florida and New York City." Anchored by four major retailers, it contains 400 stores, roller coaster, Ferris wheel, water slide, and a giant inflated comic strip character. The Mall's general manager estimated that during the two-year period following its opening, almost $400 million in sales "were to people from out of the state." According to the newspaper article, Minneapolis could be characterized as "the nerve center for a rich farming area stretching across five states and the Canadian province of Manitoba." Disregarding local patrons who would not use train service, let us now see how well Amtrak can accommodate Mall visitors from the surrounding territory.

Duluth, the second largest metropolitan area in Minnesota, enjoyed one daily Twin Cities round trip (the morning Badger northbound and afternoon Gopher southbound) immediately before Amtrak's start-up. At various times since, Amtrak's Arrowhead or North Star has served Duluth. The city now has no rail passenger service. Travelers from Milwaukee (the largest city in Wisconsin) have only the Empire Builder, a train that arrives in the Twin Cities at 11:10 P.M.; returning, they depart at 8:20 A.M. These times are perhaps not so bad, considering that a few years ago, the westbound train arrived after midnight. For North Dakota, the state capital of Bismarck has had no service since the demise of Amtrak's North Coast Hiawatha. Residents of Fargo, considered a large municipality in this low-population state, must depart at 2:38 A.M. and return home at 4:35 A.M. Weekend trips, however, were no longer feasible after the Empire Builder ceased operating daily west of the Twin Cities. Des Moines, the capital and largest city in Iowa, has never had Amtrak service. Neither has the fifth state, South Dakota. Winnipeg, the metropolis of Manitoba, lost its Twin Cities trains at Amtrak's start-up.

Accordingly, except for Milwaukee and some smaller cities along the way, it is difficult to imagine how visitors from the five-state area plus Manitoba can conveniently use rail service to the Mall of America. Another missed opportunity.

In August 1995, sometime-presidential candidate Ross Perot presided over a three-day political "issues conference" in Dallas. National leaders of both major political parties were present. The estimated attendance, assembled from all over the nation, ranged between three and four thousand. A scattering of those attending were interviewed by the *Dallas*

Morning News. We do not know these persons' itineraries, but let us see how easy it would have been for them to have ridden Amtrak to this northern Texas metropolis.

A California interviewee, who in years past enjoyed two direct Dallas routes (*i.e.*, approaching via Midland and Lubbock, respectively), would have been forced to use Amtrak's circuitous path through San Antonio in South Texas. An interviewee from Florida, who at one time could have traveled through New Orleans and either Shreveport or Houston, did have Amtrak service available via the latter point, but it required lingering there overnight to await an outbound connection.[51] A Michigan interviewee, who previously could have chosen among several alternatives connecting through Memphis, Kansas City, or St. Louis, had available only a single Amtrak train, leaving from Chicago. When East Coast interviewees arrived at the midwestern gateways, they too would have faced these obstacles. Additionally, all of Amtrak's Texas trains had the dubious distinction of operating only triweekly. Finally, Oklahomans were totally thwarted from using rail service by that state's long-ago severance from the national passenger network.

Readers of this volume are invited to speculate as to how many of the several thousand persons attending the Dallas conference could have adapted to the above-described schedule inadequacies, either on the way there or on the way back. More missed opportunities?

A November 23, 1995, article in *The Post and Courier* (published in Charleston, South Carolina) reported that a sizeable number of out-of-state tourists visiting nearby coastal resort communities move permanently to such areas upon their subsequent retirement. One particularly popular spot is Myrtle Beach, situated within reasonable driving distance of the rail station at Florence. Considering both the preretirement tourist travel and the postretirement trips to see families and friends back home (and vice versa), Amtrak would appear to have a golden opportunity to cash in on this phenomenon.

So what has Amtrak been doing? For a number of years, the carrier's timetables noted that a local transportation authority operated a dedicated "shuttle van" connecting Myrtle Beach with the daylight Palmetto at Florence. This arrangement facilitated Amtrak's sole through service linking this burgeoning coastal resort with the remainder of the nation. In 1990, the timetable reference abruptly disappeared without explanation; because nothing took its place, the public must presume that Amtrak was no longer interested in Myrtle Beach customers. The timetable does inform us that no rental cars, which might have been used as substitutes for the van, were available in Florence. Although a national

---

[51] Later, Amtrak withdrew from the Houston-Dallas corridor. Passengers transferring from the Sunset Limited to the Texas Eagle (or vice versa) were then forced to go all the way to San Antonio.

bus carrier maintains a limited Florence-Myrtle Beach schedule, lack of coordination with the trains probably convinced a number of travelers to go entirely by bus. Another missed opportunity.

Later, Amtrak continued in its downsizing mode by terminating the Palmetto.[52] The remaining Myrtle Beach passengers that this train still carried after the apparent demise of the van—who somehow found alternate means of making their way from/to Florence—were then forced onto the nighttime Silver Meteor (but only, of course, if its space were not already sold out on a given day). In the southbound direction, that train dumped these passengers in Florence at 3:57 A.M. If they desired to complete their journey to Myrtle Beach by bus (leaving in midmorning), they had the dreary options of (1) checking into a hotel shortly before sunrise for an abbreviated rest, or (2) "cooling their heels" at some all-night diner. Local acquaintances who might be expected to offer a lift would have to be exceptionally dear souls to agree to pick them up at that outrageous hour. To be frank, most of the former Myrtle Beach travelers likely forsook Amtrak completely at this point. Another missed opportunity.

While we are discussing South Carolina, it should be mentioned that the famous Spoleto music festival in Charleston attracts 100,000 persons each spring. According to *The Washington Post* of May 27, 1995, reaching that city was more difficult because "airlines have cut back on flights." This author—who resides not far from Amtrak's Alexandria, Virginia, station (served by Charleston-bound trains)—has never been exposed to any promotional material touting whatever convenience the carrier believes it can offer Spoleto festival-goers. Another missed opportunity.

Looking west, a traditional tourist spot attracting even more sightseers these days is Los Angeles. The *Washington Post* of May 25, 1995, reported that this city was "near the top of many vacationers' lists this summer, and according to local tourism officials, one reason is the [O.J. Simpson] trial and the daily exposure it gives the city on national TV."

In the same year in which Los Angeles tourism was seen climbing, Amtrak reduced its Chicago-Los Angeles Desert Wind frequency from daily to triweekly. Although the Southwest Chief continued to operate daily between these points, travelers from important intermediate stations (Omaha, Denver, Salt Lake City, Las Vegas, etc.) found their service reduced by more than half. Another missed opportunity.

Moreover, the same newspaper reported on May 15, 1995, that Oklahoma City had engaged a New York public relations firm to promote tourism and business growth in this state capital. Local interests were seeking to exploit an upcoming $240 million program that would provide

---

[52] It remains to be seen whether subsequent introduction of the Silver Palm, now operating on a similar schedule over the Florence route, offsets any of the enmity that Amtrak brought on itself in South Carolina (and other states) by discontinuing the Palmetto.

"new parks, expanded convention and performing arts centers, new sports venues and other amenities." Having discontinued the Lone Star, Amtrak was not positioned to share in the increased travel that the municipal project was expected to generate. Another missed opportunity.

In Louisiana, according to a December 3, 1995, article also appearing in the same newspaper, recently opened riverboat casinos at Lake Charles and Shreveport/Bossier City were "attracting hordes" of Texans traveling to these spots for short-stay visits. Although such travelers could reach the respective points on the Sunset Limited and the Texas Eagle (the latter in conjunction with a sixty-three-mile Amtrak Thruway bus connection), the triweekly schedules applying to both these trains precluded, for example, weekend trips.

Daily service would, however, likely attract a goodly number of casino-bound travelers, although the relatively short distances from the principal high-population Texas cities to the two named Louisiana stations do limit Amtrak's revenue potential. Nevertheless, to the extent that these persons could occupy unneeded space vacated by other eastbound passengers disembarking from the two Los Angeles-originated trains in such places as Houston and Dallas (and similarly, on their way home in the opposite direction, occupy space reserved by Texas-boarding passengers headed west), Amtrak could increase its casino-related revenue without incurring the cost of adding extra coaches. Another missed opportunity.

Back east, a 1995 central Pennsylvania tourism study concluded that although "organized tour groups currently ride Amtrak trains in measurable numbers [and] the National Park Service also has a summer program of on-board ranger interpretation...these programs are not directly targeted to the...large numbers of existing visitors at nearby attractions [which constitute] a potential market large enough to fill all the available Amtrak seats between Johnstown and Altoona if marketed effectively. This excursion service has the potential to develop a yearly ridership of 58,700 people [and the] new excursions would use existing Amtrak service and would require limited startup funding."

Speaking specifically of Amtrak's Pennsylvanian, the study observed that the "existing schedules and capacity are nearly unknown to the general public [and that] aggressively presenting Amtrak as a publicly accessible alternative for a low cost impulse-buy excursion is not done today." Another missed opportunity.

On a different subject, the Federal Aviation Administration released an interesting document a while back. It is called the *1994 Aviation Capacity Enhancement Plan*. Consisting of 362 pages printed on ultraexpensive paper, this publication placed a value upon commercial aircraft delay, and outlined planned airport and airway improvements believed capable of reducing it.

In the appendix thereto, Table A-1 displayed the 100 largest U.S. airports, ranked according to the number of 1992 "enplanements."[53] The first fifty of these airports are listed in Table 5 below. Although comparable data for rail passengers are not readily available, there is also shown in Table 5 the number of weekly Amtrak train departures for which boarding is allowed. The Amtrak figures, applicable to late 1996, are depicted on a weekly basis to eliminate confusion arising from less-than-daily train service in some cities. Thruway bus departures are not included in these counts.

Table 5
Comparison of Air and Rail Service

City (Airport)	Annual Emplanements	\multicolumn{10}{c}{Amtrak Train Departures Per Week}

City (Airport)	Annual Emplanements	0	6	9	11	12	14	17	21	26	More
1. Chicago (O'Hare)	29,986,963										O
2. Dallas-Ft.W (Int.)	25,963,239		O								
3. Los Angeles	22,911,585										O
4. Atlanta	20,966,165					O					
5. San Francisco	15,257,138	O									
6. Denver (Stapleton)	14,476,601						O				
7. New York (Kennedy)	13,363,580										O
8. Miami	12,587,255							O			
9. Newark	11,967,280										O
10. Detroit	10,986,668										O
11. Phoenix	10,958,400	O									
12. Boston	10,641,027										O
13. Minneapolis/St. Paul	10,639,045				O						
14. St. Louis	10,476,785										O
15. Honolulu	10,220,760	\multicolumn{10}{c}{≈≈≈≈≈≈≈≈≈Not Applicable≈≈≈≈≈≈≈≈≈}
16. Las Vegas	10,038,181	O									
17. Orlando	9,989,092										O
18. New York (LaGuardia)	9,751,311										O
19. Pittsburgh	9,350,221										O
20. Charlotte	9,099,577										O
21. Houston (Intercon.)	8,977,522	O									
22. Seattle-Tacoma	8,773,365										O
23. Philadelphia	7,850,375										O
24. Washington (Nat'l)	7,331,346										O
25. Salt Lake City	6,510,001						O				
26. San Diego	5,923,072										O
27. Cincinnati	5,780,241	O									
28. Washington (Dulles)	5,308,389										O
29. Nashville	5,068.011	O									
30. Raleigh-Durham	4,939,336										O
31. Tampa	4,793,304						O				

continued

---

[53] Although "enplanements" is not defined in the document, the term presumably refers to passengers boarded, including those changing domestic commercial flights, as well as those using private aircraft and international flights.

Table 5
Comparison of Air and Rail Service (continued)

City (Airport)	Annual Enplanements	0	6	9	11	12	14	17	21	26	More
32. Baltimore	4,370,829										O
33. Cleveland	4,266,092										O
34. San Juan	4,192,629	≈≈≈≈≈≈≈≈≈Not Applicable≈≈≈≈≈≈≈≈≈									
35. Ft. Lauderdale-Hollywood	4,109,796								O		
36. Houston (Hobby)	4,008,376	O									
37. Memphis	3,958,432				O						
38. San Jose	3,775,332										O
39. Kansas City	3,697,821										O
40. Portland	3,589,361										O
41. New Orleans	3,340,961								O		
42. Oakland	3,186,437										O
43. Indianapolis	3,139,728		O								
44. Ontario	3,042,508		O								
45. Dallas (Love)	2,944,942		O								
46. Santa Ana	2,769,936										O
47. San Antonio	2,730,976			O							
48. Albuquerque	2,626,486						O				
49. Sacramento	2,552,734										O
50. Palm Beach	2,514,095								O		

An examination of Table 5 reveals that Dallas-Fort Worth International Airport, with the second largest number of enplanements of all U.S. airports, serves (together with Love Field, the forty-fifth) a metropolitan area that had but six train departures in an entire week. That amounts to an average of fewer than one per day! Similarly, Las Vegas, Houston, Cincinnati, Indianapolis, and Ontario (with enplanements numbered sixteenth, twenty-first, twenty-seventh, forty-third, and forty-fourth, respectively) also had just six weekly train departures.[54] Nashville, the city with the twenty-ninth largest airport in terms of enplanements, had no Amtrak trains at all.[55] More missed opportunities.

Interestingly, Columbus, Ohio (with the sixteenth largest U.S. city population and the twenty-ninth largest U.S. metropolitan statistical area in the 1990 census), was fifty-second in 1992 enplanements. It would appear then that Columbus, location of the state capital and primary state university, as well as significant commercial activity, was comparatively underserved by air carriers. Pathetically, not only does Amtrak fail to seize advantage of the partial void by competing aggressively in this market, it chooses not to compete at all. Another missed opportunity.

---

[54] Ontario had twelve departures if one counts the consolidated Sunset Limited and Texas Eagle as separate trains.

[55] While San Francisco and Phoenix (numbered 5th and 11th, respectively, in enplanements) had no Amtrak trains, they were at least connected to nearby stations by Thruway bus.

Finally, the author will share with readers a recent personal experience. In the summer of 1995, he conceived a circular multiple-stop journey to see friends in Akron, Ohio, and in the central Minnesota lake district, as well as to visit the luxury resort at French Lick Springs in Southern Indiana and Mammoth Cave National Park in central Kentucky.

None of these four places seems particularly exotic. At one time, Akron enjoyed multiple arrivals by passenger trains of three Class I railroads (Baltimore and Ohio, Erie, Pennsylvania); certain Twin Cities-Pacific Coast trains of both Northern Pacific and Great Northern once provided a variety of schedules through central Minnesota; Monon formerly served French Lick directly, while Baltimore and Ohio advertised the availability of taxicabs from/to its main-line Mitchell, Indiana, station; Louisville and Nashville conveniently stopped at Cave City, gateway to Mammoth Cave.

However, this trip was made by automobile because a train itinerary covering these places was no longer feasible. The author did not possess sufficient boldness to ask his Ohio and Minnesota friends to meet postmidnight arrivals of the Broadway Limited and the Empire Builder, respectively. That, coupled with the points in Indiana and Kentucky having lost all accessibility to the rail network, foreclosed a journey on Amtrak. Another missed opportunity.

Chapter VI
Evaluating the Demand For Rail Passenger Service

In the preceding chapter, we lamented the inability of many travelers to use Amtrak's meager network in reaching their destinations. Before embarking upon our plan to design an optimal route system (which comes in Chapter VII), let us examine the role that many see for the passenger train in today's society. Readers will observe that people all over the country regard current or potential rail service as a logical means for fulfilling their transportation needs. Collectively, such people create the demand for trains, not only within their respective regions, but also as part of a larger national network.[56]

Let us begin by acknowledging that the tourism industry promotes the unique appeal of rail service. For example, in a nine- by four-inch advertisement placed by an Atlantic Coast resort in *The Wall Street Journal*, fully one-third of the space features a photograph of a smiling couple alighting from an Amtrak sleeping car. Below the picture is a narrative of the travel experience awaiting a rail vacationer to this spot.

The text begins with a description of a typical trip down from New York: "You can get on the train in the afternoon...and sleep through 'til morning. About breakfast time, you'll be in Yemassee, South Carolina. We'll be waiting to take you to beautiful Fripp Island..." After being tempted with tantalizing references to fishing, swimming, beachcombing, golf, and tennis, readers of this upscale newspaper were urged to call Amtrak's toll-free number for a train ticket. In fine print, the advertisement notes that air passengers can be met at nearby Savannah, Georgia, but it is clear from the tone that the resort is championing use of Amtrak.

While this particular advertisement was not Amtrak-sponsored, the carrier should recognize that promoting overnight sleeping car travel can

---

[56] Implicitly underlying the manifestations of passenger demand identified in this chapter is an assumption that Amtrak's pricing policy correctly gauges the elasticity of demand for the various market strata.

provide long-term payoffs. As reported in an earlier issue of *Modern Railroads* (March 1958, at page 100), a public survey revealed that whereas a majority of travelers had never tried first class rail, those who had done so like it and "return again and again." Chances are that if a similar survey were made today, the new results would not be greatly different.

Detractors of rail passenger service frequently say that young people as a group shun trains. An article in the *Los Angeles Times* of April 23, 1995, suggests otherwise. The railroad involved was Metrolink, the regional carrier in Southern California. According to the newspaper, five hundred "lovers" departed from the Lancaster station one recent Saturday night to celebrate the Palmdale High School senior prom being held seventy-seven miles away at the Biltmore Hotel in downtown Los Angeles. One 18-year-old student in a blue-black tuxedo gave his approval: "Cool."

Of course, one round trip on what is basically a commuter railroad does not necessarily confirm a pattern. Amtrak would be foolish, however, if it did not see latent demand arising from this pleasurable evening. Association of the train ride with an "air of romance" (as the newspaper put it) should be good for repeat business on the rails. Imagine transforming Amtrak trains in California—and elsewhere—into modern versions of the storied Orient Express, with all its romantic intrigue.

But rail passenger service is more than pleasure travel. A January 13, 1996, article in *The Columbus Dispatch* reported that the Ohio Rail Development Commission, after initially toying with a possible multibillion-dollar high-speed rail project, announced it would recommend the legislature go forward with financing "basic passenger trains." Characterized as capable of serving 75 percent of the state's residents, such trains would operate Cincinnati-Cleveland (via Dayton, Springfield, and Columbus) and Pittsburgh, Pennsylvania-Toledo (via Cleveland).

According to the commission's executive director, these trains were designed for (1) business people presently traveling by automobile, but who wish to work en route; (2) the elderly; and (3) drivers unwilling to "fight the traffic." Although the article did not say so specifically, if Amtrak were selected as the operator, it would be reasonable to expect the national carrier to schedule its existing trains to connect with the new service at common points.

While the Ohio planners had satisfied themselves that sufficient demand existed to justify government support, inauguration of the trains might be deferred pending start-up of a new commuter rail project being designed to connect Canton, Akron, and other communities with Cleveland. According to a June 21, 1995, article in *The Beacon Journal* (published in Akron), the commuter trains might be available sometime in 1997. Both Akron and Canton travelers, having lost their Amtrak service in recent years, would then be able to rejoin the national network at Cleveland.

Meanwhile, the *San Francisco Examiner* for August 13, 1995, reported that the Butte County Association of Governments was planning to return daylight passenger trains to certain Northern California points now served only in the middle of the night by Amtrak's Coast Starlight. In the Sacramento vicinity, they would connect with existing trains to provide single-day rail journeys as far as Bakersfield in the southern portion of the San Joaquin Valley. A senior officer of the group noted that the service should benefit "commuters, tourists, and travelers in general." Implementation of the new trains would be governed by further studies of station locations, etc.

In Missouri, the *St. Louis Post-Dispatch* of September 3, 1995, reported that obtaining state funding to reinstate the Mule (a St. Louis-Kansas City train discontinued by Amtrak with little advance warning the previous April) was no problem. Citizen demand had resulted in the train's being back in operation by July.

Moreover, according to that newspaper, Amtrak discontinuances in 1995 so alarmed people around the country that "Congress started hearing from constituents. The result? A congressional budget resolution that retains Amtrak's operating subsidy level through 1999."[57]

On the East Coast, the Department of Transportation of the state of New York embarked upon a "policy and planning effort...that meets travel needs of our citizens...." A 1994 document, *New Directions*, acknowledged that "Amtrak rail passenger service provides downtown-to-downtown connections between New York's major cities and Montréal, Toronto, Chicago, and Boston." The draft of a 1995 transportation plan titled *The Next Generation: Transportation Choices for the 21st Century*, listed various "action steps," including an upgrading of "rail passenger service between Buffalo, Albany, and New York City ... [that] will help relieve highways and airports in New York State at or approaching capacity ...."

A *Railway Age* article published in the April 1995 issue revealed at page 45 that "Several prospective new regional and intercity passenger rail services are seriously considering the application of diesel railcar technology...." The specific intercity services mentioned were Scranton, Pennsylvania-Hoboken, New Jersey (133 miles) and Portland, Oregon-Eugene (125 miles). The magazine also noted that another intercity service, for which the roadway is already being upgraded to 79-m.p.h. standards, is the 112-mile Boston-Portland, Maine, line now scheduled for locomotive-hauled equipment. While these three routes are shorter than Amtrak's average passenger trip, all connect with the existing long-distance network, although not at the same station in each instance.

---

[57] The Kansas City-St. Louis route was included in a list of eleven state-subsidized Amtrak routes identified in a June 22, 1995, *Wall Street Journal* front-page article dealing with efforts of states to offer customized, intercity rail passenger service within their borders.

On March 15, 1996, Amtrak divulged plans to purchase high-speed tilt trains for its heaviest-density route, *viz.*, Boston-New York-Washington. The announcement was carried on nationwide television news broadcasts. When this equipment enters service, it will undoubtedly engender further widespread publicity. Assuming that technical expectations are met, ensuing public acceptance will likely result in renewing general interest in Amtrak's long-distance network by persons not having recently patronized such trains. A major question is, will Amtrak be ready for an upsurge in business? History suggests that it may not.

In this connection, readers are invited to consider a study undertaken in the 1980s by Ronald C. Sheck, Ph.D., then-associate professor of geography and planning at New Mexico State University (Las Cruces) and currently a program manager at the Center for Urban Transportation Research at the University of South Florida (Tampa). Professor Sheck's study, titled *Amtrak 90: A Route to Success*, was prepared to demonstrate how a quality, nationwide rail passenger system could ultimately recover all operating costs and contribute toward future capital investment needs. More will be said about Professor Sheck in Chapters VII and VIII, but it is pertinent to note here his observation that Amtrak itself had acknowledged it could not accommodate the full demand for rail passenger transportation.

Specifically, Professor Sheck showed that by Amtrak's unofficial estimates, it turned away more than 1.5 million would-be riders in the summer of 1980 because of insufficient space. These disappointed people amounted to 7.1 percent of the 21.2 million passengers which the company's trains carried that year. Presumably, Professor Sheck's figure excluded many more persons who had long before given up on Amtrak because of its historic configuration and capacity inadequacies. Moreover, considering the subsequent increase in U.S. population, comparable figures today may be a great deal higher.

Before this chapter on demand for passenger train service ends, something should be said about the accuracy of assertions expressed by the General Accounting Office (GAO) in its reports to Congress. On page 50 of a 1978 report titled *Amtrak's Subsidy Needs Cannot Be Reduced Without Reducing Service* (CED-78-86), GAO noted that although the company had made "extensive capital expenditures on new and refurbished equipment...[t]he small percentage increase in the number of people Amtrak serves does not seem to be proportionate to the Nation's investment."

As this author sees it, a problem with GAO's interpretation is that it ignored the private railroads' minimal capital expenditures for equipment in the years immediately preceding their 1971 departure from the business. A significant portion of Amtrak's early car acquisitions that so concerned GAO was a "catch-up" for cyclical equipment replacement the private railroads had failed to make in the late 1960s.[58] Under the circumstances, to criticize the level of passengers, as compared with the number of seats provided in new cars, borders on disingenuousness.

---

[58] Professor Sheck also made such an observation. In his words, "The nearly $1 billion spent by Amtrak on new passenger cars and locomotives over the past decade has replaced worn out equipment, but it has not provided any opportunity for significant growth."

Chapter VII
A Proposed Amtrak Network

This chapter incorporates an effort to delineate an optimal long-distance passenger train network. It proposes specific services for operation over defined routes. Such a network strikes a balance between an adequate national system serving major population centers or international gateways and a reasonable subsidy covering shortfalls from passenger fares and other income sources. For rail lines not presently accorded Amtrak service, it may be necessary to clarify common-carrier obligations through appropriate legislation.

Public acceptance of the system as a viable transportation alternative requires a sensible frequency of departures/arrivals. Generally speaking, such a proposition demands morning and afternoon trains for the shorter distances, and daylight and overnight trains for medium distances. Some long-haul services merit multiple routes between common end points to provide sightseeing diversity and to serve intermediate stations. Overnight trains should be timed, when possible, to attract business travelers. (Today's timings in this regard are, for the most part, terrible. One could ask if Amtrak sales personnel even attempt to solicit corporate patronage.)[59]

Throughout this chapter, there is an emphasis upon connectivity, enabling inbound trains to transfer continuing passengers to outbound trains at intersecting junctions. Moreover, the schedules give consideration to efficient turnaround and servicing of equipment, and to duty time for crew personnel.

Abandonment or severe downgrading of some trackage, *e.g.*, the former Penn Central (PC) main line between Pittsburgh and Columbus, necessitated development of alternate routings. (CSX and Norfolk

---

[59] It is this author's understanding that when the Baltimore and Ohio Railroad operated its Ambassador between Detroit and the East Coast, at least one Michigan automobile manufacturer traditionally held blocked sleeping car space for its personnel traveling to Washington to conduct business with the government.

Southern have not expressed any intent to disrupt Amtrak trains operated by PC-successor Conrail following their upcoming acquisition of this carrier.) It is also recognized that such factors as reduction in track superelevation on lines of concentrated freight traffic, the high cost of maintaining power switches not required for freight trains, and growing freight volume on selected lines have hindered maintenance of some historic time schedules. Reinstatement of service at certain points requires reactivation or duplication of station facilities.

As stated in the preface, these schedules exclude high-frequency corridors, commuter runs, the Auto Train, and stub-end regional services sponsored by local governments.[60]

The proposed network reflects a curtailment from the level of rail passenger service operated before the post-World War II expansion of highway and air transport facilities.[61] Thus, the quantity of service suggested herein does not provide for transporting all persons traveling between given points. Rather, the service is tailored to those who find train travel fits their needs, consistent with the intent of offering such service where the volume of passengers is justified by significant traffic flows, including those arising from the benefits of connectivity.

Brief descriptions of the proposals follow.[62] To avoid confusion ensuing from the multiplicity of rail lines now incorporated into a number of large systems, initials of former railroad owners are sometimes used to identify routes. Corresponding timetables, showing schedules of the trains to be operated over such routes, appear in Appendix A.

1. New York/Boston-Chicago

Direct east-west service, providing morning and evening arrivals and departures, is offered via Buffalo and Cleveland. While only one of these carries through Boston cars, the other—involving a change of trains at Springfield, Massachusetts—should supply sufficient passengers for

---

[60] Ideally, Amtrak acceptance of locally sponsored trains under the Section 403(b) program should constitute neither an operational nor a financial detriment to its ability to perform basic long-distance service.

[61] For example, immediately prior to the 1958 enactment of Section 13a of the Interstate Commerce Act expediting train discontinuances, the Pennsylvania Railroad operated thirteen or fourteen (depending upon direction) daily longhaul services each way on its New York-Philadelphia-Pittsburgh line. The schedules herein propose only three such trains in each direction.

[62] For readers wishing to examine detailed engineering specifications covering certain of these routes, the author recommends (1) findings of the Interstate Commerce Commission in *Adequacy of Intercity Rail Passenger Service—Track*, 348 I.C.C. 518, 520-550 (1976); and (2) *Rail Passenger Corridors (Final Evaluation)*, a joint report to Congress dated April 1981, by Drew Lewis, secretary of transportation, and Alan S. Boyd, president of Amtrak.

Amtrak to justify reinstating a pair of its former Boston-Hartford-New York trains operating via that point. A local service also operates between Chicago and Cleveland, making Detroit and Columbus connections at Toledo.

Cleveland is a connecting point for Columbus, Dayton, and Cincinnati and for Pittsburgh, Washington, and Philadelphia. Montréal and Detroit services connect with the main line in both directions at Schenectady and Toledo, respectively.

Buffalo (Depew) is the connecting point for New York/Boston and Cleveland passengers traveling to/from Niagara Falls. VIA Rail Canada provides service beyond for Toronto and Windsor (Detroit).

All other trains on the New York-Albany-Buffalo-Niagara Falls segment would be sponsored by New York State. If the state were to support an overnight train between these points, Massachusetts may wish to propose a connecting link providing a morning arrival and an evening departure at Boston. Also, Pennsylvania and Ohio could arrange for a link connecting Buffalo with the Cleveland gateway.

2. New York/Washington/Pittsburgh-Cleveland/Chicago

Included are day and overnight services between Cleveland/Pittsburgh and both New York/Philadelphia and Washington. Consideration can be given to switching at Washington selected cars to/from appropriate Northeast Corridor trains, thus restoring the through service at Baltimore once offered by B&O (Baltimore and Ohio Railroad) and PC (Penn Central Transportation Co.)

Also, there is overnight service between East Coast points and Chicago via Akron, consolidated west of Pittsburgh. For passengers unable to use the latter direct train and passengers desiring Pittsburgh-Chicago daylight travel, alternate service is available via Cleveland, albeit somewhat slower. Some Chicago-Columbus service is offered through a connection at Fostoria.

The overnight train from New York to Pittsburgh is available to carry those Philadelphia-Lancaster-Harrisburg passengers lost when Amtrak discontinued the traditional late evening Keystone commuter run. Similarly, Washington-Pittsburgh trains are available to provide day trips to Harpers Ferry, traditionally a popular tourist stop.

If Ohio provides Canton-Cleveland commuter service as expected, Akron would also enjoy daytime connections with Chicago and Pittsburgh.

3. Washington-Montréal/Niagara Falls

This schedule includes overnight trains between Northeast Corridor points and Montréal via New London. Daylight service is available between New York/Boston and Montréal via Schenectady. Service between Vermont stations and points on the Northeast Corridor south of Springfield, Massachusetts, would be state-sponsored, as now.

Day and overnight travelers between Niagara Falls and both New York/Boston and Cleveland are handled through Buffalo (Depew).

Detroit (Windsor)-Buffalo service is available using VIA trains, with an intermediate change at Aldershot, Ontario.

4. Cleveland/Detroit-Cincinnati

Daylight and overnight service is provided. All trains to/from the northern points are consolidated south of Columbus to provide maximum service at minimum cost. If Ohio sponsors direct day service over CSX between Dayton and Toledo, such a route would allow passengers traveling from Cincinnati to points in central Michigan to arrive in Detroit in time for the late afternoon connecting train.

Columbus-Chicago passengers connect at either Toledo or Fostoria. Overnight Detroit-Chicago passengers connect at Toledo. Cincinnati and Columbus passengers to/from Pittsburgh change at Cleveland.

5. Chicago-Detroit/Pontiac

Three daytime trains operate on schedules similar to those presently in effect. An overnight service (restoring New York Central Railroad's Motor City Special at the end points) is also provided through a connection with the New York/Boston-Chicago line at Toledo.

Pontiac is served directly in each direction by one Chicago train and by one Cincinnati train operating via Toledo.

Western portions of this line are used by state-sponsored trains serving Grand Rapids and Lansing-Flint-Port Huron.

6. Cincinnati-Chicago/St. Louis

Daytime and overnight Chicago-Cincinnati trains are handled through Indianapolis. St. Louis-Cincinnati daylight trains operate via the CSX direct line; overnight service is provided over CR (Consolidated Rail Corp.) west of Indianapolis, using one locomotive set to minimize cost.

The St. Louis services provide connections for Memphis and Nashville at the various junctions shown in Appendix A.

7. New York-Miami/Tampa

Two through trains provide morning and afternoon arrivals and departures at all end points. One of these provides day service in both directions north of Columbia, South Carolina. This designated service frequency is not intended to preclude Amtrak from offering additional New York-Florida trains, with daylight service accorded Eastern South Carolina points. If not so offered, Thruway bus service connecting with Raleigh-line trains at Rocky Mount or Wilson, North Carolina, can suffice.

It is intended that overnight Raleigh-New York and Raleigh-Atlanta service (once provided by SCL's [Seaboard Coast Line Railroad] Palmland and Silver Comet, respectively) would be available, using North Carolina-sponsored trains east of Greensboro.

8. New York-Cincinnati/Birmingham/Montgomery

This route provides twice-daily service between New York and Atlanta, with one train serving Birmingham and the other Montgomery. At both of these Alabama points, connections are made with trains from/to Mobile and New Orleans. Additionally, the Birmingham line connects with overnight service to/from both Chicago and Memphis. Chattanooga and certain Florida passengers change at Atlanta.

Twice-daily Northeast Corridor-Cincinnati service is provided, using the C&O (Chesapeake and Ohio Railway) line west of Washington. One pair of trains arrives and departs both Washington and Cincinnati at times similar to those previously offered by B&O's Metropolitan Special.

Cincinnati passengers once handled on Southern Railway's Carolina Special to/from Greensboro and Spartanburg (via the remote Asheville line) connect at Charlottesville.

9. Cincinnati/Jacksonville-New Orleans

Twice-daily service is offered over the entire route, providing both A.M. and P.M. arrivals and departures at major stations. Additionally, this route forms a link in service between Cincinnati and both Atlanta and Memphis; also, it is a link in overnight service between Chicago and stations south of Nashville.

At Flomaton, the traditional junction with the L&N (Louisville and Nashville Railroad)-SCL Jacksonville line is restored. Twice-daily service provides more convenient timings at Pensacola and Tallahassee. Also, additional connections are thus offered with the New York line at Jacksonville.

10. Chicago-Jacksonville

This route provides direct service between Chicago-Evansville-Nashville to supplement alternate service via Cincinnati and Louisville. At Atlanta, it connects with trains to/from New York. St. Louis passengers are accommodated via connections at Terre Haute or Vincennes.

Because of heavy freight traffic currently moving south of Chattanooga, additional passing sidings may be needed. L&N operated one daily passenger train in each direction over this line at the time of Amtrak's start-up.

Service between Atlanta and Florida connects with New York trains at either Jacksonville or Savannah, depending upon the feasibility of joining the NS (Norfolk Southern Corp.) and CSX lines at the latter point. One-night service, once provided between Chicago and Florida, did not enjoy good connections at the northern terminal; therefore, two-night service is offered here, compensated for with arrival at Florida points earlier than the historic times.

11. Little Rock-Atlanta

This routing restores a Mississippi River crossing—at Memphis—between existing ones at St. Louis and New Orleans. It connects with St. Louis-Texas trains at Little Rock. East of Memphis, it offers service to/from Louisville and Cincinnati (via Nashville) and Atlanta and Birmingham (either direct on the schedule of SLSF's [St. Louis-San Francisco Railway] Sunnyland or via Nashville).

12. Chicago-St. Louis/New Orleans

Services are offered thrice-daily on the St. Louis line and twice-daily on the New Orleans line. The state of Illinois may desire to sponsor additional Springfield trains.

Memphis-St. Louis service is offered through connections at Effingham or Odin.

13. Chicago-Winnipeg/Seattle

Thrice-daily service is offered in the Chicago-Twin Cities market, once served by several private railroads. Perhaps at least one train in each direction can operate on BN (Burlington Northern Inc.) via East Dubuque, Illinois, to gain passengers lost when Amtrak previously withdrew from Dubuque, Iowa.

Between the Twin Cities and the West Coast, there were four trains operating at the time of Amtrak's start-up. The two suggested here constitute a reasonable compromise. Whether they are split between the GN (Great Northern Railway) and NP (Northern Pacific Railway) routes, thus restoring service to central North Dakota and Southern Montana, is subject to determination. If Winnipeg can be served (reasonably, with the cooperation of VIA within Canada), the existing Empire Builder route via Grand Forks perhaps can be moved to BN's Surrey cut-off.

BN's once-idle Stampede Pass line between Spokane and Seattle (which *The Journal of Commerce* for January 24, 1996, reported would be reopened) may be available for one of these trains if clearances allow. It could concomitantly serve the central Washington tri-city area.

14. St. Louis/St. Paul-Kansas City/Omaha

These routings provide Kansas City with service thrice-daily on the St. Louis line and twice-daily on the Twin Cities and Omaha lines. For the first time, Des Moines has Amtrak service and the Twin Cities has noncircuitous service to/from Omaha, Lincoln, and Denver. When the CRIP (Chicago, Rock Island and Pacific Railroad) and CB&Q (Chicago, Burlington and Quincy Railroad) railroads' pre-Amtrak passenger trains both served the connecting point of Chariton, they used separate stations one mile apart; however, Amtrak did not see this an impediment in its evaluation of the connection, as discussed in Chapter II, subchapter 7.

Overnight Chicago-Omaha service analogous to CB&Q's Ak-Sar-Ben Zephyr is provided in connection with the second transcontinental service proposed to operate via Kansas City.

15. Chicago-Denver/Fort Worth/Albuquerque/El Paso

The eastern portions of the Chicago-California service are included herein. Since Topeka is to be served by a new service operating via El Paso and Southern Arizona, the present Southwest Chief would use the time-saving Ottawa Junction bypass. At Newton, that train would connect with service to/from Oklahoma and Texas; at La Junta, it would connect with ATSF's (Atchison, Topeka and Santa Fe Railway) Denver line via the resort city of Colorado Springs. Because of decreased maximum speed limits, discontinuance of some intermediate stops between Newton and La Junta may be necessary to maintain schedules unless the 1996 reroute east of Galesburg (Cameron) proves faster.

According to the March 25, 1996, issue of *Traffic World* at page 24, new intermodal freight traffic will be emphasized between Pueblo and Denver. ATSF operated a daily passenger train in each direction over this line at the time of Amtrak's start-up. Planned capacity improvements, including restoration of a portion of one track removed sometime ago, would benefit both intermodal and passenger traffic.

Fort Worth-Kansas City and Fort Worth-Denver services are consolidated south of Newton to avoid incurring the cost of the former Texas Zephyr route via Amarillo. Oklahoma City-Denver through car service, previously provided on ATSF's Antelope and Centennial State, can be restored.

The El Paso routing requires two nights, instead of the three used by Amtrak's Texas Eagle, between Chicago and Los Angeles. Since the Topeka-El Paso portion of this route was earlier rehabilitated by SSW (St. Louis Southwestern Railway), there should be no insurmountable difficulty in maintaining the schedule of the former Golden State. (See Chapter I, subchapter 1.)

Overnight Chicago-Omaha passengers are handled via Kansas City. Since a set of equipment would otherwise lay over in Omaha all afternoon—and available time does not allow, *e.g.*, a Sioux City turn—the state of Nebraska may wish to sponsor an Omaha-Lincoln-Omaha daylight round trip at a very low incremental cost. CB&Q once offered comparable timings as part of a Chicago-Denver operation.

16. Denver/Albuquerque-Portland/Sacramento/Los Angeles

To expedite Chicago-Portland service, UP's (Union Pacific Railroad) traditional Granger-McCammon shortcut is reactivated for passenger trains. Direct Pacific Northwest-Salt Lake City service is maintained, however. With a change of trains in Pocatello, a second Denver-Salt Lake City route becomes available to supplement the DRGW (Denver and Rio Grande Western Railroad) line.

So that the train to Portland may be more assured of connecting with the overnight service to the San Francisco Bay area, it may be necessary to use the main freight line bypassing the Boise station. While unfortunate, it is believed that the Portland connection is more vital.

Amtrak's service between Denver and California is retained. While UP's historic weekend trains between Los Angeles and Las Vegas are desirable today, such an operation should be conducted on a regional basis. Reno should also have regional service from/to the San Francisco Bay area.

17. St. Louis-Forth Worth/Houston/San Antonio

The traditional splits accorded the overnight Texas Eagle at Longview and Palestine are restored. Additionally, daytime service is operated via Marshall between Fort Worth and both Memphis and New Orleans.

Service to/from the latter point can directly serve Baton Rouge if KCS (Kansas City Southern Railway) is used east of Shreveport. New Orleans-Kansas City passengers previously handled on the latter route would connect through St. Louis, with only moderately greater elapsed times than those of the former Southern Belle.

Little Rock-Chicago service is available via either St. Louis or Memphis, and Chicago-Fort Worth service via either Kansas City or St. Louis.

18. New Orleans-Los Angeles

These end points are connected by two trains: east of El Paso, one operates via Forth Worth/Dallas and Shreveport, the other via San Antonio and Houston. Additionally, because of the population concentration in eastern Texas, a second train is provided between San Antonio and New Orleans. SP (Southern Pacific Transportation Co.) traditionally operated both the Sunset Limited and Argonaut over the latter line.

Between Houston and Dallas/Fort Worth, one train is offered. It connects with both the Kansas City and Denver services handled via Oklahoma City and Wichita. This Texas market appears large enough for additional schedules; however, since it is intrastate, other trains should be locally sponsored.

West of El Paso, the route handles passengers transferring from/to Chicago and Kansas City. Intermediate stations on the Los Angeles line include the popular stop at Tucson, where SP previously originated a Chicago sleeper.

19. Seattle-Sacramento

This route has the one long-distance Denver/Texas train (north of Portland) and two long-distance California trains. Amtrak is enabled to use one or both of the latter for inaugurating the earlier plan to handle passengers' automobiles on the West Coast. (See Chapter II, subchapter 3.)

It is proposed to handle existing Coast Starlight passengers en route to/from southern California via San Joaquin Valley trains at Martinez. Thus, a reasonable arrival time southbound at Sacramento is allowed; as was done traditionally, this overnight service terminates in Oakland (and originates in Oakland northbound). If the state of California desires to sponsor a southbound coast route train on a schedule similar to SP's Noon Daylight, there could be an Amtrak connection with it in Oakland or San Jose.

Seattle-Vancouver, British Columbia, and Seattle-Eugene, Oregon, local service would be operated on a regional basis.

20. Oakland/Sacramento-Los Angeles

Between these end points, there is both a night train along the coast and an inland daylight train on a schedule similar to that operated until Amtrak's start-up. It is understood that UP is reluctant to resume passenger service over the Bakersfield-Palmdale portion of the latter route, since to do so would assertedly interfere with central California freight trains en route to/from the big West Colton classification yard. Metrolink passenger trains operating in the Antelope Valley use this congested section only between Palmdale and Lancaster. Accordingly, Amtrak's use of the line needs to be arranged.

Because of the demonstrated interest of the state in extending certain Santa Barbara service to San Luis Obispo, it is reasonable to conclude that it would be willing to continue to San Jose. Accordingly, passengers would not lose their present daytime coast route trains under the proposal herein.

Establishment of service over the Bakersfield-Barstow line reconstitutes a portion of ATSF's San Francisco Chief. Having a second Chicago-Northern California train is logical, because the California Zephyr reportedly cannot accommodate all passengers. Also, the ATSF route is the quickest for Kansas City passengers, and it offers Oklahoma and Texas connections at Newton, Kansas. In years past, ATSF regarded the San Francisco-Houston market sufficiently important to warrant through service, then operated through the Clovis, New Mexico, junction.

Postscript on the Twenty Route Descriptions

On April 30, 1971, the private (pre-Amtrak) railroads operated 49,533 total route-miles in passenger service. By contrast, the long-distance schedules proposed herein encompass 30,061 route-miles. Of this number, 26,363 or 87.7 percent (1) were adopted from the private railroads' network at the time of Amtrak's start-up, (2) comprised a portion of the national carrier's system during part or all of its first twenty-five years, or (3) both. Thus it can readily be seen that the suggested network does not constitute a radical proposal. The route segments used are identified in Table 6 (on the following page):

Table 6
Proposed Route Segments, Showing Mileage

1. Boston-Chicago	1,017
2. New York-Albany/Rensselaer	141
3. New York-Pittsburgh	444
4. Washington-Pittsburgh	300
5. Pittsburgh-Hammond/Whiting	456
6. Pittsburgh-Cleveland	139
7. New York-New London	125
8. New London-Montréal	370
9. Schenectady-Cantic, Quebec	178
10. Buffalo-Niagara Falls, Ontario	31
11. Washington-Philadelphia	135
12. Berea, Ohio-Cincinnati	248
13. Detroit-Pontiac	23
14. Detroit-Columbus	179
15. Detroit-Porter, Indiana	239
16. Cincinnati-St. Louis	338
17. Cincinnati-Chicago	327
18. Indianapolis-East St. Louis	237
19. Washington-Jacksonville	753
20. Jacksonville-Winter Haven	206
21. Jacksonville-Auburndale, Florida	201
22. Lakeland-Tampa	31
23. Winter Haven-Miami	207
24. Selma-Savannah (via Raleigh)	369
25. Alexandria-Birmingham	791
26. Atlanta-Montgomery	175
27. Orange, Virginia-Cincinnati	518
28. Covington, Kentucky-New Orleans	922
29. Baldwin, Florida-Flomaton, Alabama	394
30. Chicago-Amqui, Tennessee	436
31. Nashville-Atlanta	285
32. Atlanta-Folkston, Georgia	313
33. Memphis-Bald Knob, Arkansas	92
34. Memphis-Nashville	215
35. Memphis-Birmingham	251
36. Chicago-St. Louis	282
37. Chicago-Carrollton Av., Louisiana	932
38. Chicago-Fargo	658
39. Fargo-New Rockford-Minot	234
40. Minot-Seattle	1,263
41. Fargo-Noyes, Minnesota	193
42. St. Louis-Kansas City	281
43. St. Paul-Kansas City	493
44. K. City-Pacific Junction, Iowa	175
45. Chicago-Denver	1,037
46. Cameron, Illinois-Kansas City	250
47. Kansas City-Albuquerque	903
48. Kansas City-El Paso	945
49. Newton-Fort Worth	403
50. La Junta-Denver	182
51. Denver-Salt Lake City	571
52. Salt Lake-McCammon, Idaho	147
53. Denver-Pocatello	644
54. Pocatello-Portland	714
55. Albuquerque-Los Angeles	905
56. Salt Lake-Daggett, California	623
57. Salt Lake-Sacramento	729
58. St. Louis-Fort Worth	741
59. Longview-Taylor	226
60. Palestine, Texas-Houston	151
61. Fort Worth-San Antonio	285
62. Carrollton Av., Louisiana-Los Angeles, California	1,990
63. Carrollton Av., Louisiana-Marshall	348
64. Ft. Worth-Sierra Blanca, Texas	523
65. Dallas-Houston	264
66. Seattle-Roseville	819
67. Sacramento-Oakland	89
68. Oakland-Los Angeles	463
69. Martinez-Bakersfield	283
70. Bakersfield-Barstow	138
71. Mojave, California-Burbank	91
Total	30,061

Some readers desiring a more comprehensive network will be disappointed in certain omissions from these recommended schedules. For example, no service is contemplated over a few railroads still handling long-distance passengers at the time of Amtrak's start-up: Chicago and North Western, Grand Trunk Western, Norfolk and Western (including its former Wabash component), and Northwestern Pacific. Moreover, service is not provided for such medium-size cities as Huntsville, Alabama; Columbus, Georgia; Peoria, Illinois; Muncie, Indiana; Cedar Rapids, Iowa; Lexington, Kentucky; Saginaw, Michigan; Vicksburg, Mississippi; Springfield, Missouri; Elmira, New York; Winston-Salem, North Carolina; Tulsa, Oklahoma; Knoxville, Tennessee; Brownsville, Texas; and Wausau, Wisconsin.

Despite considerable thought having been given to including the itemized communities, it seems to this author that they are located either in obscure places on secondary routes, or on lines which if served would provide unwarranted duplication of others deemed more essential. Amtrak could, of course, embrace them in some future expansion. Indeed. Professor Sheck provided for ultimate inclusion of several in his treatise.

Another matter deserves brief attention here. In pre-Amtrak days, multiple lines converging on downtown terminals sometimes served common suburban stops. Examples include Englewood (Chicago), Winton Place and Covington (Cincinnati), and Carrollton Avenue (New Orleans). Through passengers intending to make outbound connections at a downtown terminal, but prevented from doing so because their inbound train was running late, could nevertheless on occasion accomplish train-to-train transfers at a common suburban stop. Although such stops are not shown in the schedules herein, Amtrak management should consider their establishment where feasible.

It is believed premature at this point to hypothesize specific equipment assignments. However, it should be recognized that there are instances in which cars should be switched between trains at key junctions, particularly sleepers in the middle of the night. The use of road crews and power for such purpose, rather than switch engines, seems to have been made an accepted practice on Amtrak.

Although the level of patronage will vary for the trains included in the proposed network, all are interconnected such that each contributes to the value of the entire enterprise. It is important that the complete system be kept intact.

Chapter VIII
Procedure for Ascertaining Revenues and Costs

The previous chapter outlined a cohesive rail passenger network maximizing opportunities for "connectivity." That is to say, arrivals and departures in major terminals were generally scheduled to foster train-to-train connections. This process facilitates achievement of favorable load factors. High utilization is desirable because of the sizable proportion of fixed costs characteristic of the railroad industry.

Thoughts such as these are not new, and they certainly are not original ideas of this author. One of the most respected railroad leaders, the late John W. Barriger, observed on page 13 of his 1956 book *Super-Railroads* that "The problem of railway passenger service, like freight, is caused by inadequate volume—poor load factor."[63]

The principal objective of this chapter is to illustrate financial ramifications arising from the reconfiguration of Amtrak's long-distance network suggested in Chapter VII. We shall extrapolate our figures from revenue and cost data covering a sample month's operation of the Chicago-Los Angeles Southwest Chief that the company released from its fiscal year 1995 accounting records. These data are reproduced in Table 7 under the column headed "Actual."[64]

Since the more extensive schedules proposed in Chapter VII provide for enhanced connectivity, we can expect greater utilization for the Southwest Chief. Between the end terminals of this train, opportunity for intertrain connection of passengers traditionally existed only at Joliet,

---

[63] At various times the president, chief executive officer, or chairman of four Class I railroads, Mr. Barriger was regarded with sufficient esteem that he was privileged to be listed in *Who's Who in America*. So we should endeavor to heed his wisdom. That is why, unlike exhortations for service discontinuances emanating periodically from the Department of Transportation and other places, this author seeks to ameliorate Amtrak's problems through a growth in traffic volume as Mr. Barriger has counseled.

Galesburg, Kansas City, Barstow, and Fullerton. With the additional connections provided in Chapter VII, these new or expanded gateways become available: (1) Kansas City: for St. Paul, central Iowa, and Omaha passengers; (2) Newton: for Oklahoma and Texas passengers; (3) La Junta: for Denver passengers; and (4) Barstow: for direct service to/from the San Francisco Bay area. Moreover, if Cincinnati were to enjoy daily service, rather than the triweekly Cardinal, up to a doubling of connecting passengers could likely be realized from/to that city.

In this author's judgment, providing capacity for these new connecting passengers and for those persons Professor Sheck found were being turned away for lack of space could lead to enlarging the Southwest Chief's passenger load—and ticket revenue—by at least 50 percent.[65] Of course, there would be an incremental increase in costs for equipment, crew wages, dining car food, travel agency commissions, etc. The adjusted revenues and costs are portrayed in Table 7 under the column headed "Potential." Notes appended thereto explain the rationale for quantifying these data.

Table 7
Average Revenues and Costs Per Trip (Southwest Chief, November 1995)

Revenues	Actual	Potential	
1. Coach passengers	$21,080	@150%	$31,620
2. Sleeping car passengers	7,976	@150%	11,964
3. Food and beverage	4,786	@150%	7,179
4. Mail	15,179	@145%	22,010
5. Express	746	@145%	1,082
6. Baggage	82	@150%	123
7. Total revenues	$49,849		$73,978

continued

---

[64] One's first impression from analyzing the cost figures in Table 7 is that the delineation of individual items does not follow the Uniform System of Accounts first prescribed for railroads by the Interstate Commerce Commission. Rather, the costs are subdivided into three broad categories: (1) train-related, (2) system-related, and (3) route-related. Some of the assignments of particular accounts are puzzling. For example, recognizing that it is common for business firms to centralize data processing, one would think that "computer systems" would be classified as system-related. But no, this item appears in the route-related category instead. Fuel is not identified as such; yet it would constitute one of the larger cost elements.

[65] The revenue increase from the new passengers is predicated upon an assumption that the average length of trip and the ratio of first class passengers to coach passengers is not significantly different from the present.

Train-related costs
8. Engine crews	$4,555		@80%	$3,644
9. Train crews	4,658		@80%	3,726
10. On-board service crew	9,648		@120%	11,578
11. Crew support	2,461		@120%	2,953
12. Maintenance of equipment during trip	12,440		@120%	14,928
13. Heavy maintenance, wreck repair	4,017		@115%	4,620
14. Food	1,519		@120%	1,823
15. Liquor and tobacco	153		@150%	230
16. Nonconsumables	811		@100%	811
17. Commissary support	1,301		@120%	1,561
18. Payments to ATSF for on-time performance	4,302		@100%	4,302
19. Other railroad payments, costs	3,114		@100%	3,114
20. Information and reservations	2,440		@120%	2,928
21. Marketing and advertising	1,200		@100%	1,200
22. Commissions	1,201		@150%	1,802
23. Sales	763		@145%	1,106
24. Self-insurance	4,153		@123%	5,108
25. Purchased insurance	401		@123%	493
26. Depreciation of locomotives and cars	7,920		@115%	9,108
27. Other train-related costs	5,788		@100%	5,788
28. Subtotal	**$72,845**			**$80,823**

System-related costs
29. General and administrative	$2,547		@52%	$ 1,324
30. General support	1,134		@52%	590
31. Training	57		@52%	30
32. Subtotal	**$ 3,738**			**$ 1,944**

Route-related costs
33. Stations serving Southwest Chief only	$2,029		@68%	$1,380
34. Stations shared with other trains	2,883		@65%	1,874
35. Maintenance of Amtrak-owned tracks	185		@61%	113
36. Facility costs	398		@61%	243
37. Depreciation	2,280		@61%	1,391
38. Computer Systems	4,098		@61%	2,500
39. Police	118		@61%	72
40. Interest	3,277		@61%	1,999
41. Taxes	134		@61%	82
42. Transportation overhead	1,459		@61%	890
43. Equipment service center	9,026		@61%	5,506
44. Other route-related costs	1,276		@61%	778
45. Subtotal	**$27,163**			**$16,828**

46. Total all costs (L.28+L.32+L.45) $103,746 $99,595
47. Deficit per trip (L.46-L.7) $ 53,897 $25,617
48. Deficit per passenger(L.47÷349&524)$154 $ 49

Explanation of percents used to derive potential revenues and costs:

Lines 1-3, 6, 15, 22 (150%)—Revenues from passengers increase by the same rate as the increase in the number of passengers. Commissions paid to travel agencies increase under the assumption that the latter will maintain their current percentage of ticket revenue collected.

Lines 4-5, 23 (145%)—Mail and express revenues increase at a lesser rate than that for passengers because of difficulties encountered in transferring a large volume of traffic at points of intersection with other trains.

Lines 8-9 (80%)—Engine and train crew economies are realized through a shorter time away from home terminals, arising from the operation of multiple trains on certain sections of this route.

Lines 10-12, 14, 17, 20 (120%)—On-board service costs increase at the lower rate because of the ability of existing crew personnel to serve some new passengers. En route car inspection generates little incremental expense for longer trains. Food and commissary economies are realizable through reduced wastage, as more passengers use existing diners and restrooms. Information and reservations costs increase at a lesser rate than that of passengers because some of the new business will come from present Amtrak customers already possessing timetables.

Line 13, 26 (115%)—This figure reflects an incremental addition to equipment units, moderated however by shorter terminal layover time permitted through an increase in the number of trains dispatched.

Lines 16, 18-19, 21, 27 (100 %)—Items in this category appear relatively unaffected by changes in passenger volume.

Lines 24-25 (123%)—This figure reflects the lower exposure to claims on mail and express traffic, *vis-a-vis* passengers.

Lines 29-31 (52%)—An increase in the number of trains operated in the potential system would result in reduced fixed overhead items per trip.

Line 33 (68%)—The traditional Southwest Chief constituted the sole train at twenty-five of its stations. Potentially, it would do so at only seventeen.

Line 34 (65%)—Traditionally, the train served eight joint stations. Potentially, it would serve sixteen such stations, including union stations at Chicago and Los Angeles. The latter would experience marked reductions in per train costs arising from multiple trains and added routes.

Lines 35-44 (61%)—These costs, calculated on a weighted train-mile basis, are adjusted to reflect the reduction in allocations arising from the sharing of the route with new services.

Line 47—Difference between total costs & total revenues (Line 46-Line 7).

Line 48—Deficit per trip on Line 47 divided by the number of passengers. (Southwest Chief's recorded 255,000 FY1995 passengers divided by 365 days and multiplied by 0.5 to split between west- and eastbound trips equals 349 actual passengers; half again as many would be 524 potential passengers.)

By comparing the "Actual" and "Potential" columns in Table 7, we see that revenues increase from $49,849 to $73,978 (line 7). But while train-related costs rise from $72,845 to $80,823 (line 28), allocated system-related and route-related overhead costs decline (lines 32 and 45). The total per trip deficit is about halved from $53,897 to $25,617 (line 47). Finally, the deficit per Southwest Chief passenger carried is down sharply, *i.e.*, from $154 to $49 (line 48).

The advantages of connectivity enhancement, shown to improve the position of the Southwest Chief, can also work for the other train routes described in Chapter VII. In Table 8 below, we will make financial projections covering all the potential long-distance services, again starting with data furnished by Amtrak.

The mathematical progression in Table 8, lines 1, 2, and 3, develops the weighted average deficit per train-mile sustained by currently operated long-distance trains. Lines 4 through 6 show how the connectivity benefits quantified in Table 7 are used to approximate the average per train-mile deficit for the proposed long-distance service (line 7). This deficit is then applied to the projected annual train-miles (line 8), generating the aggregate potential yearly deficit (line 9). As can be seen, the latter figure is lower than the fiscal 1995 long-distance deficit in line 1.

Table 8
Potential Long-Distance Deficit

Item	Source	Amount
1. Actual FY95 long-distance deficit	Amtrak	$508,580,000
2. Actual FY95 long-distance train-miles	Amtrak	17,390,000
3. Actual FY95 long-distance deficit/train-mile	L. 1 ÷ L. 2	$29.25
4. Actual Southwest Chief deficit/trip	Table 7, L. 47	$53,897
5. Potential Southwest Chief deficit/trip	Table 7, L. 47	$25,617
6. Ratio of potential: actual deficit	L.5 ÷ L. 4	0.475
7. Potential long-distance deficit/train-mi*	L. 3 x L. 6	$13.89
8. Potential long-distance train-miles/year	Appendix A	36,190,432
9. Potential long-distance deficit/year	L. 7 x L. 8	$502,685,100

* The potential long-distance deficit in line 7 is derived by multiplying the actual long-distance deficit *per train-mile* (line 3) by the ratio of the Southwest Chief's potential deficit *per trip* to its actual deficit *per trip* (line 6). Consistency of application suggests that since the line 3 deficit is expressed on a *per train-mile* basis, lines 4 and 5 (used to calculate line 6) should also reflect *per train-mile* deficits, rather than *per trip* deficits. However, in light of Amtrak's 1996 reroute of the Southwest Chief east of Galesburg (Cameron) from ATSF to BN, application of a line 6 ratio based upon *per train-mile* deficits would create the risk of producing a distorted result for the potential yearly long-distance deficit (line 9).

Actually, Table 8 overstates the potential deficit for at least two reasons. First, the accounting data upon which the figures are based still reflect the higher costs of maintaining much of Amtrak's original diverse fleet of cars inherited from the many private railroads. As the carrier continues to standardize equipment design, unit maintenance costs will decrease. Second, the enhanced service described in Chapter VII and illustrated in Appendix A will enable Amtrak to reduce hotel expenses for passengers now stranded at intermediate junctions when arriving trains are late.[66]

The potential $502.7 million long-distance deficit in Table 8, line 9, can also be evaluated per passenger-mile and per passenger. Table 9 shows that these amounts, reflecting connectivity benefits, decrease significantly from levels actually incurred today. (Compare lines 4 with 6, and 8 with 10.) In other words, as more people use the system, the costs are spread over a greater number of passengers and the deficits are markedly reduced. This consequence demonstrates that Mr. Barriger was right: Railroads can improve load factor—and benefit society—by adding trains, not discontinuing them.

---

[66] As an example, current Detroit-bound passengers arriving in Chicago on a very late eastbound California Zephyr may miss the Twilight Limited, the final connecting train of the day to Detroit. Rather than being housed in a Chicago hotel at Amtrak's expense and not reaching Detroit until the following afternoon on the Wolverine, these passengers could use the overnight service via Toledo as shown in Appendix A. Not only do the passengers gain from a considerably earlier Detroit arrival time, elimination of the hotel expense is yet another financial benefit to Amtrak arising from improved connectivity.

Table 9
Potential Deficit Reduction Per Passenger-Mile and Per Passenger

Amount of Long-Distance Deficit	Source	Amount
1. Actual (FY95)	Table 8, L. 1	$508,580,000
2. Potential (per year)	Table 8, L. 9	$502,685,100
Per Passenger-Mile		
3. Actual long-distance passenger-miles (FY95)	Amtrak	3,154,000,000
4. Actual deficit/passenger-mile (FY95)	L. 1 ÷ L. 3	16.1¢
5. Potential long-distance passenger-miles	*	9,845,252,700
6. Potential deficit/passenger-mile	L. 2 ÷ L. 5	5.1¢
Per Passenger		
7. Actual long-distance passengers (FY95)	Amtrak	5,290,000
8. Actual deficit/passenger (FY95)	L. 1 ÷ L. 7	$96.14
9. Potential long-distance passengers	*	16,523,256
10. Potential deficit/passenger	L. 2 ÷ L. 9	$30.42

*Existing long-distance train counts increased for connectivity enhancement and addition of trains to network.

This author is well aware that anti-Amtrak forces are going to claim the bottom-line, financial projection for the potential network (line 2) is dependent upon realization of the passenger-mile and passenger forecasts (lines 5 and 9). Such an assertion is too simplistic.

To examine this matter, let us look at a railroad still having a significant passenger operation right up until Amtrak's beginnings, but whose lines today constitute only a marginal part of the latter's system. The Louisville and Nashville or L&N (since absorbed into CSX) had retained a train in each direction on its Cincinnati-New Orleans and St. Louis-Atlanta lines. It also ran a Chicago-Danville round-trip and participated (with SCL via Chattahoochee, Florida) in a Jacksonville-New Orleans operation. Contrastingly, Amtrak has settled in to using former L&N lines only for minor segments of its Cardinal and Sunset Limited routes.[67]

Passenger rail's adversaries will never countenance Amtrak use of L&N beyond this bare minimum, asserting that its planners "cherry-picked" the available trackage across the nation (from the standpoint of size of historical passenger loads) and the remainder—including most of

---

[67] For short periods, Amtrak experimented with other pieces of the L&N (*e.g.*, Louisville-Montgomery and Montgomery-Mobile) in connection with the Floridian and Gulf Breeze, trains operated primarily on other rail lines. But such experiments failed, largely because there was only limited provision for gateway connectivity.

L&N—must be summarily excluded from the network. In other words, they will say that in pre-Amtrak days, L&N-route passenger density did not measure up to the weighty traffic volumes found on some other railroads. Accordingly, running more trains on former L&N lines (as is contemplated in Appendix A) would assure heavy Amtrak losses. Let us see if such a theory has merit.

Readers will recall Professor Berge from Chapter I. Conveniently for us, Professor Berge gathered some pre-Amtrak statistics from Interstate Commerce Commission (ICC) files that will help us here. Although Professor Berge's most recent figures represent 1954 operations, older data are adequate for our purpose because they reflect an era in which the private railroads were still actively attempting to make their passenger business successful.

Anyhow, from Professor Berge's figures, embracing twenty-four railroads whose trains operated over lines forming a part of the network proposed in Chapter VII, we learn that L&N experienced a systemwide average of 60.9 passengers per train.[68] Twenty of the other twenty-three railroads in this group reported higher average loads. Of these twenty (all of which sustained system passenger deficits), seven incurred a larger average deficit per train-mile than L&N's $2.51. As to the remaining three railroads having an average passenger load lower than L&N's, two of them had a lower—not higher—deficit per train-mile.

It is apparent from the foregoing that despite comparatively modest passenger boardings, L&N was able to hold its average per train-mile deficit below that of a number of heavy-density carriers by exercising strict cost control. Notably, it did so while operating expensive sleepers and diners. Thus, we can infer from the ICC data (reflecting actual railroad cost behavior) that to the extent any initially sluggish traffic growth experienced on some routes of an enlarged Amtrak network is not compensated for by robust expansion elsewhere, vigorous cost control measures can keep the overall deficit within bounds.

Nevertheless, Amtrak remains under close congressional observation, with the expectation that most federal funds will terminate after 2002. Unfortunately, the adverse situation confronting us in the 1990s, characterized by depressed passenger boardings and the concomitant swollen per passenger deficits, is largely attributable to short-sighted

---

[68] The average number of passengers per train that L&N once experienced understates the load available to Amtrak for movement over the lines of that former carrier that are incorporated into the proposed network. That is to say, through traffic once handled between (1) Cincinnati and Memphis on B&O-IC; (2) St. Louis and Birmingham on IC; (3) Memphis and Atlanta on SLSF-SCL/SOU; and (4) Cincinnati and Atlanta, both on SOU and on L&N's Corbin Division, is available for Amtrak movement on L&N via its Nashville hub. Additionally, traffic once handled between (5) Birmingham and New Orleans on SOU, and (6) Montgomery and Florida on SCL is available for L&N movement via the Flomaton, Alabama, junction.

decisions made in the 1970s and 1980s when the Department of Transportation nearly ran the system into the ground. Had a network such as that described in Chapter VII remained in place throughout Amtrak's first quarter-century, people's travel preferences would all along likely have been reflecting a goodly use of passenger rail.

The nation must recognize, however, that ticket revenue will not sustain this service. As the private railroads said for years, albeit some of the better-off ones willingly accepted mild passenger deficits in the interest of promoting good relations with on-line communities, without public aid (or an extraordinary volume of mail and express) there will be few if any regularly scheduled trains.

Relative to defining Amtrak's future, our national transportation policy should reflect the disclosures in Chapter III regarding the failure of current highway user taxes to meet the cost of road programs (an $8 billion deficiency in 1995) and the inadequate airway user taxes (providing for a recovery rate of only 75 percent in the 1996 FAA budget). Additionally, we should give great weight to the broad popularity of long-distance rail passenger service, as substantiated in Chapter VI wherein it was noted that people across the nation pressured Congress to backtrack from a proposed Amtrak funding reduction. These factors—in addition to the crucial congestion, safety, and environmental aspects discussed in Chapters III and IV—are compelling reasons for the nation to find a way to maintain a meaningful level of rail passenger service.[69]

In evaluating the nation's options, it may be helpful to place Amtrak's financial situation into perspective:

First, for fiscal year 1995 the system deficit (about $855 million) was the equivalent of only 0.06 percent of the $1.46 trillion total federal budget for such year. In a country of 260.7 million people, that amounted to just $3.28 per capita, a minuscule sum considering that 20.7 million passengers directly benefited and countless millions more persons profited from reduced highway and airway congestion and from safety and environmental enhancements.

Second, Amtrak's operating subsidy payments from the federal treasury are likely more than offset by government revenue derived from the combination of (1) payroll taxes assessed against its employees, and (2) increased corporate income taxes paid by vendors on profits generated through the sale of supplies to the railroad. In a hearing conducted February 7, 1995, by a railroad subcommittee of the U.S. House of Representatives, Amtrak Vice-President Thomas J. Gillespie, Jr., testified

---

[69] Readers will recall Chapter IV, subchapter 2, wherein it was described how Professor Mulvey—one of Amtrak's harshest critics—conceded that the passenger carrier saved the nation (in 1970s dollars) between $28 million and $51 million annually in avoided highway accidents, and $29 million that train passengers would otherwise have spent for automobile fuel.

that in comparison with the then most recent annual operating subsidy of $392 million, tax payments by employees and vendors commonly run "between a quarter and half-a-billion dollars a year...."

Third, let us compare the deficit with other known governmental expenditures. In Fairfax County, Virginia (where this author resides), the local budget for a population of 891,000 is currently $1.6 billion. That is to say, just one county in one state lays out about twice as much for citizen services as the federal government spends on the entire forty-five state Amtrak system (direct operating and retirement act tax appropriations, plus noncash depreciation and amortization).

Before ending this chapter discussing the federal contribution, we should mention another related matter, *viz.*, the impact of our disappearing rail passenger service upon the U.S. balance-of-payments deficit with foreign nations. This deficit is frequently addressed in the financial news. Every American who has decided that a passenger train is the preferred transport vehicle for sightseeing, but who is forced to go abroad to find such service, is exacerbating the outflow of U.S. dollars.

For those readers who may be unaware of its existence, the author calls attention to *The International Railway Traveler*. Published in Louisville by The Society of International Railway Travelers, this magazine carries interesting stories on passenger railroads around the world. Using the certified distribution of approximately 4,000 copies per issue, let us do some arithmetic.

Suppose that each year, one-fourth of the family units reading the magazine decide that Amtrak's skeletonized service is not suitable for their tourism needs.[70] To keep the numbers simple, we will assume that this amounts to 1,000 couples without children. So they buy a copy of one of Thomas Cook Ltd.'s two consolidated rail timetable publications (either the continental guide covering Europe, or the overseas guide comprising the remainder of the world) and plan a three-week itinerary. Based upon standard prices charged for tourist services, these 1,000 couples contribute an estimated $9.75 million to this nation's yearly balance-of-payments deficit.[71] So far, that is not a lot of money, relatively speaking. But there is more to consider.

We should not delude ourselves into thinking that foreigners, who in nearly every other civilized country in the world have extensive rail passenger service, will be as likely to come here as tourists if they cannot get around our country in the manner in which they are accustomed to

---

[70] This number is merely for illustration. Indications are that there is an enormous untapped market for Americans desirous of taking rail tours. The author was recently a guest at the Swiss Embassy in Washington which presented a celebration of that nation's 150th anniversary of its railroad network. The embassy auditorium overflowed with enthusiastic people willing to go overseas if that is what it takes for them to find alternatives to Amtrak's meager offerings.

traveling. Every time a European tourist chooses to visit Japan or vice-versa, rather than come to the U.S., foreign money that otherwise would be spent here goes elsewhere and we forfeit an opportunity to ease our balance-of-payments deficit. Whatever the amount of money that these foreign citizens are already diverting from this country because of Amtrak's current minuscule network (a good subject for a research project), it will climb even higher if the remaining long-distance trains vanish after 2002, when Congress is insisting that the carrier become self-sustaining.

The failure of our politicians to recognize and acknowledge that skimping on Amtrak has an adverse effect upon our balance of payments suggests shallow analysis.

---

[71] Tourist-class air travelers can expect to pay up to $800 or $900 and sometimes more for a round-trip ticket from the U.S. East Coast to Europe. The fare is likely higher from other U.S. origins and perhaps double that amount to other continents. But we will use a conservative $1,000. Let us cut this figure in half, however, on the gratuitous assumption that on successive trips, American tourists alternate between domestic and foreign carriers. We will also assume that, for example, fuel purchased by U.S. air carriers overseas is offset by fuel purchased here by foreign carriers. These couples should probably budget US$150 per night for a hotel room and at least US$100 each day for meals and incidentals. For foreign rail tickets or passes, add another US$450 per person. Finally, from this author's observations, most couples will spend about US$500 for souvenirs.

Chapter IX
Where Do We Go from Here?

Since this chapter is the last in the book, it might be helpful to begin by reviewing what has gone before. Then we will look ahead to what the government and Amtrak management might do to enhance the worth of our country's long-distance rail passenger service.

Chapter I consisted of abstracts of pre-Amtrak studies addressing a variety of passenger matters, but predominantly involving economic and legal issues. A special editorial note inserted by this author dealt with an analysis of western rail passenger operations prepared by the Stanford Research Institute for a client railroad attempting to discontinue the bulk of its long-distance service. The note revealed that (1) in a transportation corridor connecting two large cities, a small fraction of persons then traveling by air would be sufficient to completely fill a train the railroad has ceased promoting and earmarked for discontinuance; and (2) appropriate advertising can expand a train's customer base without unduly increasing the overall passenger deficit, a phenomenon confirmed by the traffic statistics of another western railroad. Another editorial note showed that SRI's comparison of rail and air operating costs incurred between the end points of the route in question was misleading because of an apparent failure to credit the train with revenues derived from short-haul passengers.

Abstracts of various government studies comprised the content of Chapter II. One section revealed how the Department of Transportation participated in defining Amtrak's original routes, as well as in scaling down the network later in an attempt to decrease the federal subsidy (with only marginal results, as it turned out). This chapter also chronicled the activities of the Interstate Commerce Commission in exposing a number of weaknesses in the DOT plans. Moreover, the chapter reviewed congressional subcommittee staff studies unmasking the mismanagement of three named Amtrak trains. Lastly, it reported on Amtrak's study of a possible network expansion, in which two potential services were projected as capable of improving the carrier's economic situation. (Neither has been established as of this writing.)

Chapter III addressed the inability of the highway and air modes to fully meet the needs of intercity travelers. Moreover, it discussed these modes' safety and environmental failings. It also demonstrated that the users and beneficiaries are paying far less than the sum necessary to reimburse the respective trust funds for federal expenditures undertaken in their behalf.

Chapter IV contained analyses of various antirail entities. For the most part, their arguments (when relevant at all) were shown to have little or no merit.

Chapter V presented a litany of travel needs for which Amtrak should be, but is not, offering a reasonable transportation alternative.

Indications of demand for rail passenger service were identified in Chapter VI. We learned how a seacoast resort actively solicited rail patrons. Moreover, various state governments have identified a need for expanded intercity operation. Upon release of federal proposals to significantly reduce current service, many travelers over the nation complained to Congress. Additionally, the chapter noted Amtrak's failure to provide capacity sufficient to handle all those persons attempting to use existing trains.

Chapter VII translated the proven and latent demand for rail passenger service into a potential network, stressing cohesiveness and connectivity of the trains proposed for incorporation into it.

In Chapter VIII, we saw how the economics of one train could be improved by enhancing its connectivity with others. Moreover, realization of such connectivity benefits enables rail service to be extended to additional travelers, while markedly reducing the per passenger-mile and per passenger deficits. Additionally, the pre-Amtrak experience of one medium-size railroad demonstrated that the size of a train's passenger load alone does not control its net earnings. It was further shown that the public expenditure of monies to maintain a rail passenger system compares quite favorably with other expenditures for commonplace governmental services. Also mentioned was the lack of recognition at high levels of government that forcing Americans to go abroad to use rail service for tourism has an adverse impact upon the nation's foreign trade balance. Similarly, foreigners with money to spend are less likely to come here as tourists if they anticipate difficulty in getting around our country.

So here we are at Chapter IX. The year 1996 marked the expiration of the twenty-five-year term specified in Section 8.8 of Amtrak's basic operating agreement with the freight carriers.[72] Different circumstances

---

[72] Readers desiring to research the first quarter-century of Amtrak's history will find the June 1996 issue of *Trains* to be of interest. (This magazine previously published passenger-oriented issues in April 1959 and June 1991.) A 1994 book, *The Amtrak Story* by Frank N. Wilner (Simmons-Boardman Books, Inc., Omaha), also provided an account of the company's history.

suggest that without new legislation, rail passenger interests may no longer be able to exercise the leverage they possessed in 1971 when the railroads generally cooperated in Amtrak's creation. Also, overhanging renewal negotiations is the question of fixing liability for accidents more definitively.

A potential change in approach sometimes debated is the contracting to outsiders of on-board dining operations. As this author sees it, there are both pros and cons. Certainly, an independent entrepreneur reimbursed on the basis of a percentage of receipts would have a powerful incentive to please train patrons. To an extent, such an incentive is lacking today. On the other hand, Amtrak management would need to establish minimum standards. That is to say, the type of dining service most desirable from the standpoint of the contractor's profits may be the least desirable type from the standpoint of the passenger's expectations. Another worrisome aspect of contracting is dealing with the chaos arising when contractors elect not to renew at expiration time and, instead, announce that they are simply going to walk away from their duties.

Other ideas also may be worth exploring. An article in the *St. Louis Post-Dispatch* for September 3, 1995, described the "Lipstick Express," a bus converted to a "rolling salon" for New Yorkers traveling to their Long Island beach homes. A Manhattan entrepreneur offers manicuring, pedicuring, hair-styling, and bikini-waxing on a 2 1/2-hour ride ending in the Hampton communities. On one trip described in the article, eight patrons were attended to. "I feel fabulous," one woman exclaimed as she scrambled off at Southampton. While applying eyeliner at 65 m.p.h. is a bit tricky, the salon operator seems to manage. Are there any ideas here for Amtrak?

One concept that this author believes Amtrak may have abandoned without sufficient effort is the "economy sleeper service" offered on its Washington-Cincinnati Shenandoah in the mid-1970s. The idea was to provide a limited number of berths with bedding, but without expensive porter service. In this manner, an entire sleeping car need not be provided on lower-demand runs, but neither are passengers relegated to conventional coach service for overnight travel. Although arrangements would be necessary for servicing such accommodations, imaginative managers should be able to make the concept successful. With the recent demise of slumbercoaches, latent demand for this service may be substantial. We may look for guidance to Europe, where the couchette accommodation remains popular among budget-minded travelers.

If this author headed Amtrak, he would appoint a high-level executive whose sole responsibility would be to work within the railroad industry to improve certain trains' deplorable timekeeping performance. While late-running trains were not unknown in the pre-Amtrak era, part of the current problem is that the contract railroads' top managements no longer have the traditional incentive to showcase their companies' proficiency through operation of a well run passenger service. And, of course, low priorities accorded Amtrak in the executive suite filter down to positions directly affecting passenger train operation, *e.g.*, dispatchers.

Timetables must strike a proper balance between determining normal transit times, and providing excessive padding so that trains are never late. When chronic delays are experienced, the causes should be systematically identified and addressed. (Some of the present lateness is Amtrak's own fault, of course.) Although possible solutions such as passing sidings consume precious capital, once the funds are spent, every Amtrak train thereafter operating over the particular line benefits.[73]

Another frustration arises from the recent disappearance from the *Official Railway Guide* of the complete fare quotations and tariff rules. This publication, available in many libraries, has served as a valuable reference in travel planning. Amtrak should recognize that while its own ticket office personnel and commercial travel agents usually may access essential data electronically, its customers typically cannot do so. Moreover, only very simple questions lend themselves to efficient answering through the toll-free telephone number.

On another subject, this author has heard of passengers customarily packing personal window cleaning devices for use at station stops. While here again there are concerns such as finances and labor unions, perhaps mid-run window cleaning is an ideal job for contractors.

Readers may wish to ponder another question. The complimentary newspaper distributed to first class passengers frequently turns out to be *USA Today*. Perhaps the explanation is that Amtrak's far-flung network enables it to obtain a volume discount. However, attention is called to the subject of newspaper quality, as expressed in a July 31, 1995, opinion article, a portion of which is reproduced here by express permission of the publisher:

> Leaving aside a couple of tabloids such as the *News* and *Post* in New York, there are essentially only two models available. One model is represented by *USA Today* and its imitators. These papers rely on the heavy use of color, short and easy-to-read stories, a heavy dose of sports, columns of news briefs, lots of how-to information and bland opinion pages. Their entertainment value is emphasized.
>
> The other model—an upscale, serious product—is represented by the *New York Times*, *The Washington Post*, the *Los Angeles Times*, the

---

[73] In its May 9, 1994, issue, *Traffic World* reported on page 34 that Amtrak President Thomas M. Downs had begun a "quarterly scoring" of the freight railroads in order to encourage them into delivering his passengers on time.

Wall Street Journal and a handful of other metropolitan dailies. They try to entertain as well as inform, but information is their principal selling point. To succeed, they require a critical mass of affluent and well educated readers found in sufficient quantities only in a limited number of markets.

—Richard Harwood, © *The Washington Post*

It is respectfully suggested that many first class passengers agree with Mr. Harwood's views. Moreover, of all the Pulitzer Prizes awarded in early 1996, Amtrak's favorite newspaper earned zero.

This author does, however, wish to commend the company for recent changes in the Capitol Limited operation (reported earlier in the semimonthly publication *Rail Travel News*), whereby first class passengers are now accorded special tables in the dining car. This is a forward step, coming long after such passengers lost the traditional Pullman Company lounge cars once assigned to a number of pre-Amtrak streamliners.

Unfortunately, there may still be instances where first class cars are positioned in trains between coaches and the diner, thus creating a lot of noisy walk-through traffic. On trains where the sleepers are located up front and mail/express cars at the rear (not an uncommon practice now), first class passengers experience louder locomotive whistle blasts than previously. At stub-end terminals where arriving trains back in, placement of sleepers at the head end may also mean, unhappily, that their occupants have the longest walk between train and station. Not backing the train in, however, subjects all passengers to diesel fumes and loud engine idling as they walk past the locomotive to reach the station.

From time to time, various persons advocate turning the entire long-distance service over to the states for operation. Former Congressman Jim Slattery of Kansas, questioning the secretary of transportation in a 1985 House hearing on Amtrak, critiqued the idea with such wisdom that his remarks are worth repeating here:

Congressman Slattery: We are looking at less than one-tenth of 1 percent of our total Federal Budget—less than one-tenth of 1 percent. It seems to me the option then is, if we have to shuttle this all back to the states, then they are going to have to raise property taxes, raise sales taxes, and raise income taxes. They are going to have to set up some kind of bureaucratic nightmare to administer all this stuff either in the Northeast Corridor or even in our own State of Kansas. How are we going to determine what the Kansas subsidy for Amtrak is going to be? What if Kansas says, "We are not going to participate." Then what kind of problems do we get into?

Secretary of Transportation: It [the train] ain't going to stop in Kansas....

Congressman Slattery: What if it has to fuel in Newton...then what are we going to say, don't let any passengers on here? This is the kind of administrative hassle and nightmare that we are going to create...that doesn't make sense. I am really struggling, frankly, with this whole concept.

Later in the same hearing, Indiana Gov. Robert D. Orr (both an Amtrak director and chairman of the Transportation, Commerce and Communications committee of the National Governors Association) testified:

The current debate over Amtrak's future is serving to discourage Amtrak management at all levels and will eventually undermine the morale of every Amtrak employee.... [I]n recent weeks there have been suggestions to the effect that the loss of Federal support for Amtrak could be replaced by subsidies from the States.... I believe that notion is best described as fanciful. It simply won't work. It isn't practical.... [O]ne result would be the balkanization of the national rail system.... [S]everal trains would no doubt be discontinued, and their demise would have an adverse domino effect upon the remainder of the system.... [T]he discontinuance of one train deprives the remaining trains of its connecting traffic.... Amtrak makes sense because it is a national system. It is an appropriate national responsibility....

Today, twelve years after the foregoing remarks were expressed in a congressional hearing, the sentiments remain equally apropos.

Appendix A
Proposed Long-Distance Network Timetables

Descriptions of the long-distance train services provided in the following twenty timetables appeared in Chapter VII. Principal stations are shown herein. Arrival and departure times are expressed as of the nearest quarter-hour. Certain cities that switched time zones in the post-World War II period (*e.g.*, Louisville and Indianapolis) are labeled with the current zone to eliminate the potential for confusion. Running times between stations take into account speeds reflected in schedules published for 1996. (Amtrak should, of course, strive to obtain faster schedules where possible.) Times shown in italics refer to trains whose schedules are primarily included in other timetables. At major terminals, simultaneous arrivals or departures are proscribed to avoid undue strain upon station resources. The schedules, all providing daily service, generate an annual total of 36.2 million train-miles.

Timetable 1

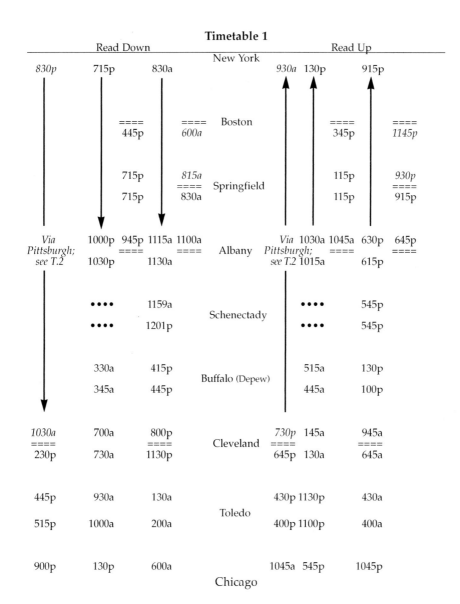

133

Timetable 2

	Read Down				Read Up			
				New York				
830p		115p	745a		930a		200p	900p
1015p		300p	915a	Philadelphia	745a		1215p	730p
1030p		315p	930a		730a		1159a	715p
1230a		515p	1130a	Harrisburg	530a		1000a	515p
1245a		530p	1145a		515a		945a	500p
	==== ====		====	Washington	==== ====			====
	1100p 430p		945a		700a 1100a			700p
645a	630a 1130p 1115p	530p	515p	Pittsburgh	1115p 1130p	345a	400a 1115a	1130a
	=== ====	====	====		====	====	====	====
715a	1201a	545p			1045p	315a		1100a
1030a		900p		Cleveland	730p		745a	
====		====			====		====	
230p		*1130p*			*645p*		*645a*	
						1130p		
	330a			Akron				
Via	330a	*Via*		*Via*	1130p	*Via*		
Toledo;		*Toledo;*		*Toledo;*		*Toledo;*		
see		*see*		*see*		*see*		
Table 1		*Table 1*		*Table 1*		*Table 1*		
	515a			Fostoria		930p		
	515a					930p		
900p	915a	*600a*			*1045a*	415p	*1045p*	
				Chicago				

134

Timetable 3

	Read Down					Read Up			
					Washington				
	345p	215p	430a	430a		1245p	645p	115a	115a
	600p	415p	630a	630a		1030a	430p	1115p	1115p
					Philadelphia				
	600p	415p	630a	630a		1030a	430p	1115p	1115p
	745p	545p	800a	800a		845a	300p	945p	945p
	====	====	====	====	**New York**	====	====	====	====
	830p	715p	830a	830a		800a	130p	915p	915p
	1130p					500a			
					New London				
	1130p					500a			
		See	See	See		See	See	See	
		Tbl. 1	Tbl. 1	Tbl. 1		Tbl. 1	Tbl. 1	Tbl. 1	
	515a					1100p			
					White River Junction				
	515a					1100p			
			1159a	1159a				545p	545p
			==========	**Schenectady**	====	====			
			1215p	1201p				530p	545p
	1100a	630p	See		530p		1115a	See	
	=====	====	Table	**Montréal**	====		====	Table	
			1					1	
	330a	415p			515a		130p		
	====	====	**Buffalo-Depew**	====		====			
	500a	430p			945p*		115p		
	615a	545p			745p		1115a		
				Niagara Falls (Ont.)**					

* Direct Connection available if New York State sponsors overnight service.
** Operated by VIA to/from Toronto, with Windsor (Detroit) connections at Aldershot.

Timetable 4

Read Down			Read Up	
		Cleveland		
1145p	1100a		600a	415p
====	====	Pontiac	====	====
400p*	630a		745p	130a*
445p*	715a		700p	1245a*
==== ====		Detroit	==== ====	
900p 230p	800a		700a 1130a	645p
1045p 415p	945a		515a 945a	500p
====	Toledo		====	
1115p	1015a		500a	430p
1159p	1100a	Fostoria	415a	345p
1201a	1100a		415a	345p
245a 145a	200p 1245p		230a 300a	115p 200p
====	====	Columbus	====	====
345a	215p		215a	100p
515a	345p	Dayton	1245a	1130a
530a	345p		1245a	1130a
700a	515p	Cincinnati	1115p	1000a

* Through train to/from Chicago (see Table 5).

Timetable 5

Read Down					Read Up			
				Chicago				
1045p	615p	200p	730a		1159a	445p	930p	*600a*
								↑
Via Toledo see Tables 1 & 4								*Via Toledo see Tables 4 & 1*
↓								
700a	1245a	830p	200p	Detroit	730a	1215p	500p	*900p*
====	====	====			=========			====
	1245a		700p*		715a*		445p	
	130a		745p*	Pontiac	630a*		400p	

* Through train from/to Cincinnati (See Table 4).

Timetable 6

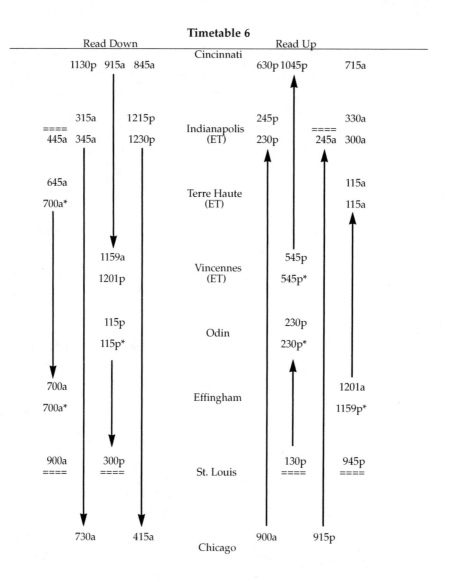

* St. Louis trains connect at Terre Haute or Vincennes for passengers traveling from/to Nashville (see Table 10) and at Odin or Effingham for passengers traveling from/to Memphis (see Table 12). Alternate overnight service between St. Louis and Memphis available via connection at Little Rock (see Tables 11 and 17).

Timetable 7

Read Down					Read Up		
				New York			
800p	430p	800a			1045a	930p	*815a*
945p	615p	945a		**Philadelphia**	900a	745p	*630a*
945p	615p	945a			900a	745p	*630a*
1159p	830p	1159a		**Washington**	645a	530p	*415a*
1245a	900p	1230p			615a	500p	*345a*
							↑
Via							*Via*
Greensboro;	1100p	230p		**Richmond**	415a	300p	*Greensboro;*
See							*See*
Table	1115p	245p			400a	245p	*Table*
8							*8*
↓							
1159a*		630p		**Raleigh**		1100a	*515p**
=====							====
		630p				1100a	
		1030p		**Columbia**		700a	
		1030p				700a	
						↑	
		600a		**Charleston**	900p		
		600a			900p		
		↓					
		800a	1245a	**Savannah**	715p	430a	
		800a	1245a		715p	430a	
	1030a		300a	**Jacksonville**	415p		145a
====		====			====	====	
1115a	1100a	345a	330a		400p	415p 1245a	100a
					↑	↑	
500p		930a		**Tampa**	1045a	730p	
====		====			====	====	
↓		↓					
	730p		1159a	**Miami**		800a 415p	

* Overnight service between northeast Corridor points and Raleigh incorporates a 403b train connecting with the New York-Atlanta line at Greensboro (see Table 8).

Timetable 8

Read Down					Read Up		
				New York			
800p	1230p	*345a*			815a	715p	*315a*
945p	215p	*530a*			630a	530p	*1245a*
				Philadelphia			
945p	215p	*545a*			630a	530p	*1230a*
1159p	430p	*800a*			415a	315p	*1015p*
====		====		Washington		=====	
1245a	500p	900a			345a	230p	1000p
300a	715p	1115a			100a	1145a	715p
====				Charlottesville	=====		
300a	745p	730p	1115a		100a	1100a	1130a	715p
	215a		545p			430a	115p
				Charleston			
	215a		545p			430a	115p
	730a		1100p			1145p	815a
	====		====	Cincinnati		=====	====
700a		1115p			930p	715a	
				Greensboro			
700a		1115p			930p	715a	
900a		100a			715p	500a	
				Charlotte			
900a		100a			715p	500a	
245p		630a			200p	1130p	
				Atlanta			
330p		700a			130p	1045p	
630p					830a		
====				Birmingham	====		
		1000a			500p		
				Montgomery			

Timetable 9

Read Down			Read Up	
		Cincinnati		
730p	900a		800a	945p
1030p	1159a		500a	645p
		Louisville (ET)		
1045p	1215p		445a	630p
145a	315p		1145p	130p
		Nashville		
245a	345p		1100p	115p
700a	800p		700p	845a
		Birmingham		
730a	815p		645p	815a
945a	1030p		430p	600a
		Montgomery		
1015a	1045p		415p	545a
			↑	↑
====	====	**Jacksonville** ====	====	
400a	500p		1230a	200p
730a	830p		815p	945a
		Tallahassee		
730a	830p		815p	945a
1159a	1230p		300p	430a
		Pensacola		
1201p	1230p		300p	430a
↓	↓			
130p 100p	230a 145a		115p 145p	245a 300a
====	====	**Flomaton**	====	====
145p	245a		100p	230a
330p	430a		1130a	100a
		Mobile		
330p	430a		1130a	100a
700p	800a		830a	1000p
		New Orleans		

141

Timetable 10

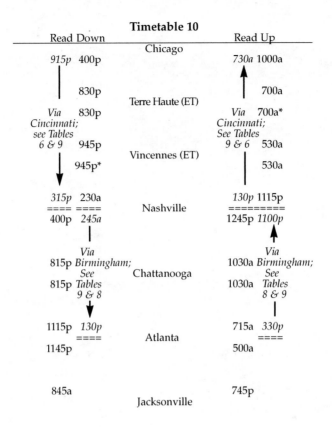

Read Down			Read Up	
		Chicago		
915p	400p		*730a*	1000a
	830p			700a
		Terre Haute (ET)		
Via Cincinnati; see Tables 6 & 9	830p		*Via Cincinnati; See Tables 9 & 6*	700a*
	945p			530a
		Vincennes (ET)		
	945p*			530a
315p	230a		*130p*	1115p
====	====	Nashville	=========	
400p	245a		1245p	*1100p*
	Via			*Via*
815p	*Birmingham;*		1030a	*Birmingham;*
	See	Chattanooga		*See*
815p	*Tables*		1030a	*Tables*
	9 & 8			*8 & 9*
1115p	*130p*		715a	*330p*
	====	Atlanta		====
1145p			500a	
845a			745p	
		Jacksonville		

*Connections available at Terre Haute or Vincennes for St. Louis passengers traveling from/to Nashville and beyond (see Table 6).

Timetable 11

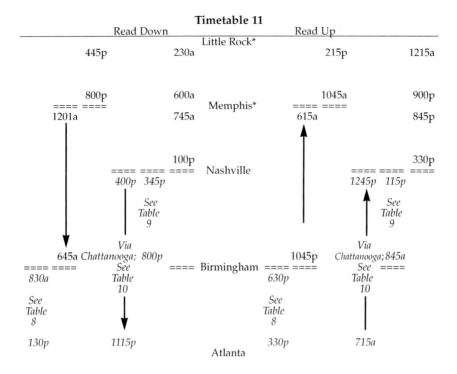

*Little Rock is a gateway both for Texas passengers and for overnight passengers traveling between Memphis and St. Louis (see Table 17). Alternate overnight or daytime connecting service between the latter points available via Effingham and Odin, respectively (See tables 6 and 12).

Timetable 12

Read Down						Read Up			
1145p	1000p	630p	100p	1015a	Chicago	630a	900a	300p	645p	945p
330a		945p	145p		Springfield	130a		1115a		545p
330a		945p	145p		Springfield	130a		1115a		545p
700a	1159p		400p		St. Louis	1115a		915a		345p
====	=====		====			====		====		====
	1230a		330p		Champaign-Urbana		615a		330p	
	1230a		330p				615a		330p	
	130a		••••		Effingham		500a		••••	
	130a*		••••				500a*		••••	
	••••		515p		Odin		••••		115p	
	••••		515p*				••••		115p*	
	845a		1130p		Memphis		1015p		715a	
	930a		1145p				1000p		645a	
	215p		430a		Jackson		530p		215a	
	215p		430a				530p		215a	
	600p		815a		New Orleans		200p		1045p	

*Daytime and overnight passengers traveling between St. Louis and Memphis change at Odin and Effingham, respectively (see Table 6). Alternate overnight service between such points available via connection at Little Rock (see Tables 11 and 17).

Timetable 13

Read Down					Read Up			
				Chicago				
	1100p		330p	1030a		615a	215p	815p
	730a	1100p	630p		930p	630a	1201p
====	====		====	St. Paul	====	====		====
915a		1115p			445p		600a	
	200p		400a		1201p		130a	
====		====		Fargo	=====		====	
200p	200p	400a	400a		1159a	1159a	130a	130a
730p		930a			630a		800p	
====		====		Winnipeg	====		====	
↓		↓			↑		↑	
1215p		115a		Spokane	845a		1145p	
1230p		145a			815a		1130p	
900p		1000a		Seattle	1100p		415p	

145

Timetable 14

	Read Down					Read Up		
				St. Louis				
500p		930a	100a		1230p		930p	600a
715p		1145a	345a		1000a		700p	315a
				Jefferson City				
715p		1145a	345a		1000a		700p	315a
↓		↓	↓		↑		↑	↑
	=====	====		**St. Paul**	====		====	
	1100a	900p			700p		845a	
	345p	145a			145p		345a	
				Des Moines				
	400p	200a			130p		330a	
	515p	••••			1230p		••••	
				Chariton*				
	515p	••••			1230p		••••	
↓	↓	↓	↓		↑	↑	↑	↑
1015p	830p	245p	700a	630a	700a	930a	400p 1100p	1201a
====	====		====	**Kansas City**	====	====	=====	
		315p	745a				330p	1000p
		730p	1159a				1130a	600p
				Omaha				

*Chariton is the connecting point for St. Paul and Des Moines passengers traveling from/to Omaha and beyond (see Table 15).

Timetable 15

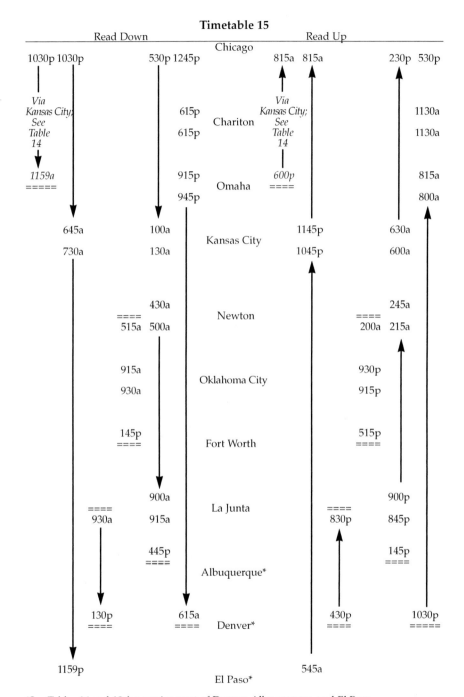

*See Tables 16 and 18 for service west of Denver, Albuquerque, and El Paso.

147

Timetable 16

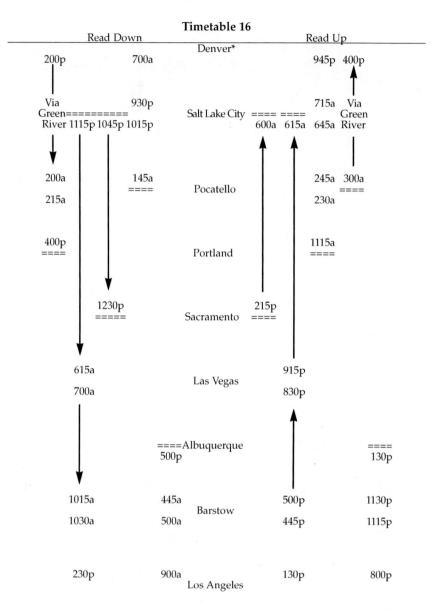

*Denver gateway available for passengers traveling on the Chicago lines (via Omaha or Kansas City/Newton/La Junta; see Table 15) or on the Houston line (via Fort Worth/Newton/La Junta; see Tables 18 and 15) to/from California and the Pacific Northwest or intermediate points. See Table 19 for Seattle service.

Timetable 17

Read Down			Station	Read Up		
From Memphis see Table 11 ==== 230p	500p	445p / 1230a / 100a	**St. Louis** / **To Memphis see Table 11** / Little Rock	800a *1230p* / 1230a / 1159p		To Memphis see Table 11 ==== 430p
630p ==== 700p* / 730p / 730p	*Via Kansas City; see Tables 14 & 15*	500a / 500a / 530a ==== 600a 545a	**Marshall** / **Longview**	1230p ==== 1159a* / 1130a / 1130a	800p / 800p / 730p ==== 700p 715p	*Via Kansas City; see Tables 15 & 14*
1030p ==== 1045p 315p**		900a / 915a	**Dallas**	845a ==== 830a 330p** 400p	415p	
1159p 430p 145p ==== ==== ==== 445p		1030a ====	**Fort Worth**	715a 215p 245p ==== ==== ==== 200p	515p ====	
==== 815a		745a / 800a	**Palestine**	==== 445p 500p	515p	
		1115a ====	**Houston***		130p ====	
930p / 930p	1159a / 1201p		**Austin***	915a / 915a	130p / 130p	
1159p	230p		**San Antonio**	645a	1100a	

*From/to New Orleans (see Table 18).
**From/to Houston (see Table 18).
***Daytime passengers traveling from Austin to Houston change at San Antonio, with a 3 1/4-hour layover at that point (see Table 18).

Timetable 18

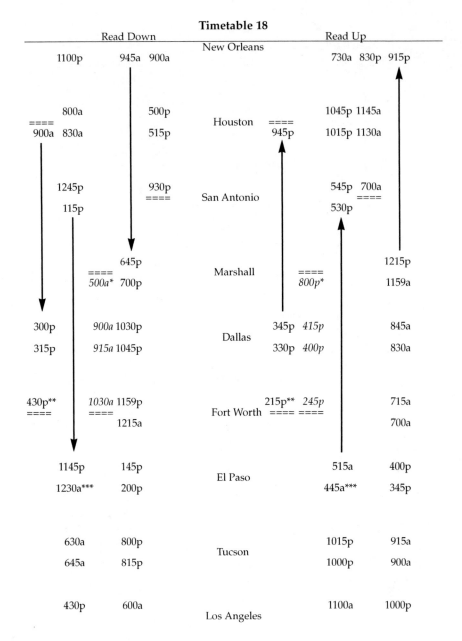

*From/to St. Louis (see Table 17).
**Fort Worth gateway provides direct Houston-Seattle service via Newton, Denver, and Portland (see Tables 15,16, and 19).
***Connection at El Paso provides direct Los Angeles service from/to Chicago via Kansas City (see Table 15).

Timetable 19

Read Down				Read Up		
			Seattle			
1000p	1215p	700a		745a	330p	845p
1100p	115p	800a		645a	230p	745p
			Tacoma			
1100p	115p	800a		645a	230p	745p
200a	415a	1100a		345a	1130a	445p
		=====Portland*		====		
215a	430p	To Houston		300a	1045a	From Houston
445a	700p			1201a	745a	
			Eugene			
445a	700p			1159p	745a	
530p	745a			1145a	730p	
			Sacramento**			

*For service between Portland and Denver-Newton-Houston, see Tables 16, 15, and 18.
**For service between Sacramento and Martinez-Oakland-Los Angeles, see Table 20.

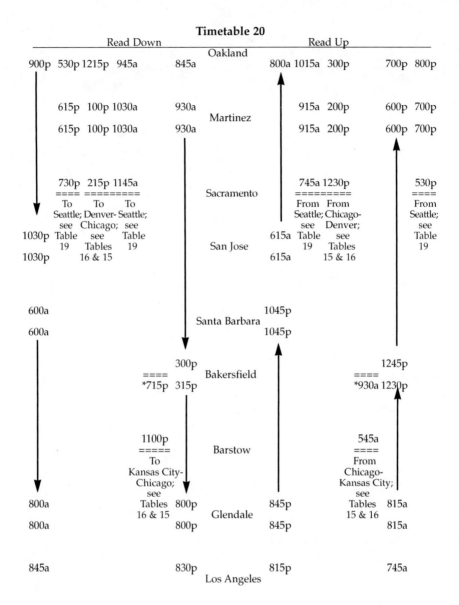

*Direct Oakland-Bakersfield connection by 403 (b) service.

Appendix B
Overview of Foreign
Rail Alternatives for Tourists

Many American tourists have discovered that a passenger train can be the ideal sightseeing vehicle. Rail passengers risk neither the burden of dealing with mechanical breakdowns nor the hazards and fatigue associated with driving on unfamiliar roads during inclement weather. They are not cramped into the tiny seats typical of buses and airplanes. Food and beverages served in style are frequently available throughout a train journey. And how much scenery can people really see from a plane thousands of feet in the air?

For those disheartened by the diminished rail passenger service in the U.S. (and Canada and Mexico, too), there is no need for despair. It is nice to have Amtrak around, such as it is, particularly for those of us whose Northeast Corridor service is partially subsidized by the remainder of the country. But overseas, there are seemingly endless possibilities. Foreign travel veterans may find little that is new in the passages to follow. Nevertheless, the writer believes that sharing his experiences with novices may help make their transition from familiar surroundings a bit less daunting. Happy reading!

1. Europe

After attempting over the years to learn some basic French, I simply had to begin my first overseas venture in France. And it met all expectations. One of my few complaints is that there seems to be an excess of American tourists, too many of the loud-talking variety. A little tip to help one blend in with the French: Wear subdued colors, nothing bright.

In Paris, my wife and I have discovered quaint hotels on both the right bank *(la rive droite)* and left bank *(la rive gauche)* of the Seine River. For our most recent visit, we chose one in the middle, on the charming Île St. Louis. Popular attractions lay within walking distance, just beyond each of the several connecting bridges. Getting around the remainder of the city is simple, too; multiple-day transit passes are valid on both the subway and buses, the routes of which are easily grasped from a good map. One learns to identify local landmarks with particular neighborhoods *(arrondissements)*.

As to the delicate French cuisine, our experience has been that most restaurant fare is superb. For breakfast *(le petit dejeunér)* Americans should get accustomed to such light items as bread and preserves *(pain et confiture)*, cheese *(fromage)*, grapefruit juice *(jus de pamplemousse)*, and sometimes a boiled egg *(oeuf)*. Note that the French do not butter their bread, and that they mix warm milk—not cream—with their coffee. American tourists visiting in springtime have the added treat of ordering something generally unobtainable at home, *viz.*, fresh white asparagus *(asperge)*.

Custom calls for menu prices to include a gratuity. Consequently, when departing a restaurant, it is acceptable to leave behind only a few coins from the change. Also, take care that you do not step on one of the many dogs one sees lying next to their masters' tables.

Now since this is a book on rail transportation, let us talk about European trains. At the outset, it should be recognized that although the famous Trans-Europ Express (TEE) service has been phased out, frequent high-speed operation is more extensive than our own.

Ticketing practices are similar to those in the U.S., except that sometimes seat reservations are obtained at a separate window. On the trains, tiny cards are placed in appropriate spots to alert other passengers not to occupy reserved seats between specified points. On occasion, passengers' names are imprinted on these cards. From station platforms, it is easy (in many countries, but not all) to quickly identify the class of car from the colored stripe painted above the windows: yellow for first, green for second.

While the newer day coaches are beginning to resemble those in the U.S., traditionally European railway cars have contained compartments with seats for six or eight passengers, depending upon the class of service. Most older cars have windows large enough to allow extending one's head outside, a common practice in stations.

You should try to distinguish uniforms between those worn by train conductors and those of customs and immigration personnel. Following adoption of the Maastrict Treaty, stamping of passports at borders has become rare. Nevertheless, it is still common on overnight journeys to surrender one's passport to the car attendant.

Sleeping cars are similar to ours, although bottled water is furnished for drinking. In Germany, the customary practice of using down-filled quilts for bedding is also observed on trains.

Some trains crossing between France and Spain (the latter a country using a broad track gauge) are fitted with special axles allowing wheels to quickly slide into the proper position. Passengers entering the former Soviet Union may experience delay while entire wheel assemblies are exchanged to accommodate the wide gauge used there and in neighboring Finland. During the days of East European communism, we observed soldiers at border points inspecting behind ceiling panels and under bunks where potential escapees could be hiding.

One aspect in which European travel amenities lag behind ours is the provision of escalators to reach track or station level. In a very few locations, weight-activated belts adjacent to stairs help in moving luggage.

Where can one travel on trains? The answer is just about anywhere. A favorite of the Europeans is the Côte d'Azur resort area in the South of France along the Mediterranean Sea. This author was captivated by the small town of Juan-les-Pins. Located a bit east of Cannes on the SNCF[74] main line, it has a sand beach (unlike Nice and certain other locations where the beaches are decidedly rocky) and a minimum of high-rise buildings. Another sand beach is found in the luxury French nudist resort of Cap d'Agde—a short taxi ride from the Agde train station—where clothes are never necessary, even in the grocery or in the bank.

Fascinating experiences await. We have climbed a twelfth-century tower in Bologna, Italy, and walked through the Czar's palace in St. Petersburg, Russia. In Gdańsk, Poland, we saw the immense shipyard where there once toiled a simple electrician destined to become the country's president.

Most people know about the great cities of Europe, but there are many smaller places equally delightful to visit. A favorite spot of this author and his wife is the peaceful village of Flåm in Norway's fjord country, where arriving trains descend a steep grade to the station at water's edge and the alighting passengers stroll to nearby guest houses, wheeling their luggage on convenient courtesy carts. In Hungary, vacation hotels on the shore of Lake Balaton are reachable by train. Also, the Spanish seaside town of Sitges is conveniently located on the RENFE[75] Madrid-Barcelona line. One can sample the variety of spots that British Rail offers, from Scottish Highland villages to charming coastal resorts at Teignmouth in Devon and St. Ives in Cornwall.

We have traveled by train through Romania (where western tourists were not particularly wanted, so we kept going) and neighboring Bulgaria (more friendly) en route to our final destination of enchanting Istanbul on the Bosphoros. Scandinavian trains cross the Arctic Circle en route to Bodø and Narvik, fishing and ore ports, respectively. This author's two rail visits to the former USSR, one before and one after the fall of communism, revealed that the once ubiquitous images of Lenin are fast disappearing.

---

[74] Société Nationale des Chemins de Fer Français.
[75] Red Nacional de los Ferrocarriles Españoles.

There is plenty to see from train windows. Amtrak travelers who enjoy Hudson River Valley scenery in the vicinity of Rhinecliff, New York (obviously named for the similarity to the cliffs lining Germany's Rhine River), can take DB[76] trains and behold the real thing. Additionally, one may ride through famous mountain passes: Brenner, Simplon, St. Gotthard. Approaching Amsterdam, passengers view huge windmills in this land claimed from the North Sea. Picturesque lakes abound in Switzerland and Northern Italy.

Moreover, one encounters practices abroad that have disappeared from North America. For example, although there is no longer a Montréal-Charlottetown sleeping car transported to Prince Edward Island by ferry, such service currently operates across the Baltic Sea and the Strait of Messina, connecting the European mainland with Scandinavia and Sicily, respectively.

And there are novel delights to be experienced on board. For example, have you ever been served a quail-egg salad, as I was on a 1995 British Pullman trip between London and Manchester?

2. Asia

Japan has the most service, with routes on all its major islands. Since this author's 1989 visit, the two principal long-distance stations in Tokyo have been joined by a through rail line, thus allowing easier connections in this capital city. Here is a bit of information for Americans using Tokyo taxicabs: Drivers, who wear white gloves and have immaculate vehicles, commonly refuse tips.

We hear a lot in the news about crowding in Japanese public transport facilities. However, the highest class of rail service (denoted green) is quite comfortable. On a holiday evening return to Tokyo from a short visit to the countryside, my wife and I did spend forty-five minutes squeezed into a vestibule with fellow passengers. But it was a learning experience and not really as bad as it sounds.

One can ride the famous Bullet trains to various places. We traveled by this means for an overnight stay in the old capital of Kyoto. Unfortunately, clouds concealed Mt. Fuji, located on this route. Later we continued by train through Hiroshima to the west coast port of Shimonoseki.

Rather than fly from Japan to South Korea, this author recommends the overnight ship. One can view the scenic coastlines of both countries before arriving the next morning in Pusan. There was only mild rolling in the middle of the strait; berths are comfortable.

---

[76] Deutsche Bahn (the new name for the combination of railway systems once operated by the Federal Republic of Germany and the German Democratic Republic).

The principal Korean rail line runs between Pusan and Seoul. There are a number of trains from which to choose. Moreover, westerners will find the on-board food service acceptable. (We were not brave enough, however, to try the dried squid available throughout the country from sidewalk vendors.)

Americans desiring a "taste" of Chinese rail passenger service, without committing themselves to long journeys, can arrange one-day round trips to Guangzhou through Hong Kong travel agencies. Complete city tours include sightseeing and lunch. Our English-speaking Chinese guide, although personable, availed himself of the opportunity to lecture us on the "marvels" of communism. There are many facilities for tourists in Hong Kong, including branches of big American banks. The situation may change after mid-1997, of course, when this traditional British colony is under the control of Beijing.

Moving now to Thailand, we recommend a short rail trip out of Bangkok on the former line to Burma that crosses the River Khwai, using a bridge made prominent in World War II. The area of the crossing is a tourist center, offering small-craft boat rides on the river itself. Although we did not do this, it is also possible to take an overnight train from Bangkok to a point on the Mekong River, just across from the Laotian capital of Vientiane, reached by ferry.

We did, however, travel by train all the way from Bangkok to Singapore, pausing in Malaysia for a two-night stay on Penang Island, a taxi ride away from the mainland railway station at Butterworth. One can make an en route stopover in Malaysia's modern capital, Kuala Lumpur. Singapore, a highly developed city-state, offers excellent tourist facilities. As information to prospective travelers entering Singapore, dogs sniff luggage for contraband. (I have also seen such dogs on the pier at Harwich, England, meeting incoming ships from the Netherlands.)

Our next country on this journey, the Philippines, seems to have just about gotten out of the intercity railway passenger business. Manila does have a suburban train network, however. Our only venture away from the city was a boat cruise to the war museum on Corregidor Island.

Finally, the last point on our trip (other than two days in Hawaii on the way home) was Taiwan. Persons wishing to make a round trip from Taipei to the big port city of Kaohsiung may do so in one day. For a relaxing trip reminiscent of a visit to Yosemite Park in California, we recommend a day journey to the famous Taroko Gorge, a taxi ride away from the Hualien railway station. On the evening return train to Taipei, we ordered dinner at our coach seats; friendly fellow passengers were not critical of our limited ability with chopsticks.

On a separate trip, I first visited New Zealand. A short stay in Auckland on the North Island was followed by a ride to Wellington, in a carriage (their term for railway coach) with sheepskin seat covers. After overnighting here, I rode the railway-affiliated ferry to Picton on the South Island, from which a second train proceeds to Christchurch. Day rail side trips operate from such point to Greymouth—via Arthur's Pass, where one may alight in a setting similar to the North American Rockies—and to Dunedin, returning by railway bus. (Travel to the end of the line at Invercargill and return requires two days.)

Then it was on to Australia. Following a long weekend in Cairns, a subtropical resort from which one can take a boat to the Great Barrier Reef, I rode the luxurious Queenslander train to Brisbane. Australian sleeping cars have "wavy" aisles to provide extra compartment space so that made-up beds do not block toilet access, a problem in U.S. roomettes. Next, it was the day train to Sydney, alighting, however, in suburban Gosford on the picturesque shoreside commuter line. Saving Sydney sights for later, I rode overnight to Melbourne on the Southern Aurora. Here is an idea for Amtrak to consider: The latter train opens its restaurant carriage well before departure, thus allowing passengers to dine with their non-traveling guests while the train is still standing in the station. The next segment was overnight on the Overland to Adelaide with its marvelous zoo featuring kangaroo and koalas. Finally it was back to Sydney on the Indian Pacific, through the outback and the beautiful Blue Mountains. The latter area warranted a return trip on the commuter line to the resort town of Katoomba.

A tip to prevent first-time American visitors to Australia from looking ridiculous: Don't forget that, like autos on the street, pedestrians approaching revolving doors should keep left. After absorbing the many sights in greater Sydney, I broke up the long trip home with a three-night stay in Tahiti, French Polynesia.

There are other places on Asian railways, notably India, Mongolia, Siberian Russia, Indonesia. More trips are definitely on the future agenda.

3. Africa

Railways on this continent are largely remnants from Britain's colonial empire, which is not surprising since that nation was where this mode of transportation originally got started. The author and his wife have traveled over a number of routes still maintained at high standards. Except for French-inspired lines in Morocco and Tunisia, most of the trains appealing to foreign tourists run in East and southern Africa.

A country that especially attracts rail patrons is Kenya. Following some semi-rugged game park viewing in the uplands, we rode the overnight Nairobi-Mombasa train en route to a relaxing weekend at a first-class Indian Ocean resort. Service from Nairobi in the other direction—*viz.*, to Lake Victoria—is available, but not as popular because of malaria outbreaks in that area, coupled with the difficulty of the various nations bordering the lake in agreeing to joint development of its resources.[77]

Farther to the south, the original Rhodesia Railways was separated into two entities upon the creation of Zambia and Zimbabwe, with the dividing point at Victoria Falls where the line bridges the Zambezi River. A relatively recent connection extends northeastward to Dar es Salaam in Tanzania. My wife and I rode between Harare (the capital of Zimbabwe) and Bulawayo, with a continuing overnight connection to South Africa, via Botswana. We found the sleeper service satisfactory, although not offering the elegance of the famous Blue Train used later from Johannesburg to Cape Town. Incidentally, the latter point enjoys a decent commuter service that we took to reach beach resorts in Vishoek and Simonstown. Pretoria also has commuter service to Johannesburg that this author found of acceptable quality.

Nigeria, the most populous nation on the continent, and certain of its neighbors have limited rail passenger service. When terrorism subsides in Egypt, that country's Cairo-Luxor-Aswan trains should become popular again. Former east-west service across southern Africa was a casualty of the war in Angola. Similarly, the war in Mozambique led to a severing of its through service. Apparently it is still possible to make the long train journey between South Africa and Windhoek, the capital of Namibia.

4. South America

This continent, despite its enormity, has only scattered rail passenger service. It can possibly be said that the best trains are in Chile, where daily sleeping cars operate south from Santiago, the capital. At Puerto Montt, bus transportation is available to continue eastward across the Andes mountains into Argentina. This route, involving multiple lake ferry crossings, is truly a vacationers' paradise. After disappearing for a while, limited sleeping car service has resumed between San Carlos de Barioche and Buenos Aires, a two-night journey. A choice of side trips from there includes a short rail excursion to the Atlantic Ocean resort of Mar del Plata and boat service (day and overnight with staterooms) to Montevideo, Uruguay.

---

[77] British interests backed the Kenya Railways construction in the late nineteenth century because of the riches in adjacent, land-locked Uganda and the desire of the government in London to protect its Sudan settlements in the upper Nile Valley from encroachment by other colonial powers. An interesting book, *The Lunatic Express* by Charles Miller (The Macmillan Company, 1971, republished in paperback by Ballantine), chronicles the building of this railway, complete with tales of early lion attacks. Happily, the present-day Uganda Railways Corporation is currently attempting to strengthen the route through enhanced freight service, as evidenced by an impressive advertisement this author saw in the October 12, 1995, Zürich edition of the *International Herald Tribune*.

Service in Brazil between Rio de Janeiro and São Paulo seems to come and go. At various times, this route has enjoyed first class day and night trains.

Some short lines are available in tourist areas of Ecuador and Peru. However, the traditional train-to-boat connections in the latter country for cruises on Lake Titicaca into Bolivia are not currently advertised. Earthquakes have damaged other lines on the continent. The remaining rail segments are too insignificant to mention.

Afterword

Before closing this volume, the author wishes to pass along a few personal observations.

Back in the 1970s, I had occasion to ride the overnight City of New Orleans. The lounge car was fitted out with the garish purple interior color widely used in those days. Lighting consisted of several bare bulbs suspended from a heavy cord loosely stretched below the ceiling. Thankfully, such cars are long gone now. However, it is questionable how much professional design effort went into their successors. To enter one of the new lounge cars and observe a straight lineup of identically shaped tables is not particularly appealing either. The new cars used in California are better in this respect.

It is regrettable also that some of the newer coach cars have small windows, rendering viewing difficult for persons in aisle seats. Similarly, Superliner sleeper windows commonly do not extend downward to mattress level (unlike, *e.g.*, those in heritage car roomettes), thus making it inconvenient for propped-up passengers to see ground-level landmarks.

Passengers generally seem to accept the new Viewliner sleeping cars, but I think it strange that no container is provided for holding wet soap bars. This failure leads to messy lavatories. Upon introduction of the latest sleeper types, roomettes were phased out. Thus, we have returned to the old-fashioned open section concept (albeit without the high aisle curtains) in which beds are prepared upon request made to the car attendant. There can be delay in rounding up the latter, however, so passengers may now have to wait a while before retiring for the night. Also, the blue night lights traditionally offered in roomettes apparently are no longer available.

Once on the former Floridian, I noticed a supply of evening newspapers being placed on board at Nashville. After the train's departure, they were nowhere to be seen. Only upon my specific request a long time later was a copy produced out of stowage. Obviously, supervision must be exercised to assure that crews perform their functions properly. Also, Amtrak ought to determine whether car attendants should greet passengers on platforms while smoking, a practice I observed on a Pioneer sleeping car trip as recently as February, 1995.

Burlington Northern issued an operating manual May 1, 1970, titled *Rules and Instructions for Dining and Sleeping Car Employees*. Doubtless, The Pullman Company had something similar; so may Amtrak. The Burlington Northern booklet contains forty-five pages consisting of twelve "General Rules" and 471 separate "Special Instructions and Rules." On several occasions while riding Amtrak, I have seen departures from the standards formerly maintained on Burlington Northern, for example, one providing that "Use of [employees'] personal radios...while on duty is prohibited."

Some train crews intimidate through passengers from visiting station buildings in major terminals while their trains pause for servicing. There are legitimate reasons for entering the stations. It is understandable that the switching accorded the Lake Shore Limited at Albany-Renssalaer can cause confusion, and certainly no personnel wish to be reprimanded for allowing passengers to be left behind or, worse yet, injured. But consideration should be extended to experienced travelers who know how to cope. This problem has also occurred at Cleveland, where no switching is performed.

Relative to dining service, we are all aware of the need for careful expense control. Yet, when Amtrak's Silver Meteor departs from Miami during normal breakfast hours, but does not offer dining car breakfast as did the private railroads before it, one does tend to speculate whether the reason is an economic one or simply a manifestation of lackadaisical practices. (My experience goes back a few years, so I cannot comment on the current operation.)

Also, when the Lake Shore Limited timetable announces that "tray meal table service" is available from Albany-Renssalaer to Boston, one would expect lunch soon after that train's midday departure. Yet, this author was once informed that because of some incomprehensible aspect of convection oven operation, it was not then generally served until Pittsfield, only an hour and a quarter before my Springfield destination. With the necessity to keep an eye on the clock, lunch was less than enjoyable. If the midday meal is not going to be served until Pittsfield, it should not be advertised as available from Albany. This principle is applicable to other trains as well. Moreover, since the expression "tray meal" is not a common term in our everyday lexicon, Amtrak should improve upon its bland description in the timetable glossary of what this is intended to mean.

Happily, the "regional specialties" that we were told a long time ago were coming to diner menus now seem to be available on a number of trains. I do, however, fondly recall a western favorite—abalone—served on a Coast Starlight diner back in the 1970s. Considering the high price of this delicacy, a "pure" serving would have been too costly, but the provision of just a hint of such taste was very welcome. It certainly bested a vegetable choice that this author once experienced on a transcontinental journey in which only corn or peas was offered at every dinner on every diner.

In the last few years, I have used Amtrak stations in various cities, including San Francisco (serving the East Bay connecting buses) and Detroit. The former, having then been recently relocated from the Transbay Terminal to the Ferry Building, was already getting its walls marred by contact with suitcases, etc. The cheap wallboard selected simply cannot withstand the heavy use of a major terminal. It will be interesting to see if recent improvements to that facility included installation of a more suitable material. The new Detroit station also has cheap wallboard. Plastic strips on the vertical edges and a few potted plants may do some good. Time will tell how well these walls hold up.[78]

An example of a beautiful station interior, unknown to many travelers because it is located in one of Amtrak's smaller cities, is that at Utica, New York. The exteriors of some others are quite remarkable, too, although a few (Seattle-King Street, for example) have been spoiled by installation of roof-top, microwave gadgetry. Kansas City's station has an odd (but not unattractive) appearance owing to the necessity to provide elevator service between street level, where a bridge to/from downtown abuts a high bluff, and the ticket office and platforms far below. Fortunately, there is no longer the situation that once prevailed at Grand Central Terminal in New York, where a sloping floor in front of the Amtrak ticket windows meant patrons found themselves standing with one leg lower than the other.

This author finds it amazing that according to the 1996 Northeast timetable, Amtrak's big Pennsylvania Station in New York no longer has a full-service restaurant. Neither do certain other high-volume stations, *e.g.*, Philadelphia and Baltimore. However, Washington, D.C., and Portland, Oregon, have exquisite restaurants. At New Orleans, the station cafeteria serves a local favorite: red beans and rice. Los Angeles recently lost its lunch room, although the long-closed main dining facility still has tables and counters that may be observed by peeking through the glass door. The famous Santa Fe Railway-affiliated hospitality name, Fred Harvey, survives today at the Grand Canyon, but under new management.

Amtrak should do a better job of providing signage or other means to notify arriving passengers of the availability of city transit. One place that comes to mind is St. Louis, where the light-rail line stops at Kiel Center, only a block or so from the train station. Other electric trolley lines begin

---

[78] Detroit's new station derives an air of prestige from its location in the shadow of General Motors Corporation's headquarters building and the famous Fisher Theatre. Unfortunately from Amtrak's perspective, GM will soon be moving to the downtown riverfront area. It remains to be seen if the city government, rumored as the prospective replacement, will maintain the stature of the neighborhood.

near Amtrak stations in Memphis (serving downtown locations) and Tucson (operating to the University of Arizona campus).

In some cities, the nearest transit stop is far enough away from the station to be burdensome for travelers carrying heavy suitcases. There may be solutions, however. At St. Paul, for example, the ticket agent might be enabled to activate a signal notifying drivers on the nearby No. 16 bus line that there are arriving train passengers to be picked up. A short diversion to the station would consume no more than three or four minutes of bus time. Passengers should not be forced to use taxicabs. Regrettably also, Amtrak does not seem to have done all it might to enlist the cooperation of local authorities in placing wait shelters at transit stops serving train stations.

Another occasional annoyance is the lack of coin lockers or parcel checking rooms in some busy locations where one would expect to find them. An example is the popular destination of Atlantic City, a point where (until through service was withdrawn) numerous passengers used Amtrak for making single-day stopovers. Moreover, the timetable information pages should confirm the presence—or absence—of such facilities so that travelers may plan accordingly.

Upon alighting from the eastbound Sunset Limited a few years ago at Tempe, Arizona, I noticed that there was no longer a station building (only a platform), discovered that typically no taxicabs met the train, and learned that the single coin telephone available to call for one was out of order. Perhaps such problems are not of Amtrak's making, but from overhearing other passengers' comments, the company lost considerable goodwill that morning. Although Amtrak has ceased serving this location, one suspects that similar problems prevail elsewhere.

None of the above stories should imply that something nearly always goes wrong or that the author regrets his past patronage of Amtrak services. For my wife and me to have returned by air to Washington, D.C.—following a social weekend in Charleston, South Carolina—traveling on the last direct flight on Sunday would have necessitated our departing around 5 o'clock in the afternoon. Rather, the northbound Silver Meteor's post-8 P.M. schedule through Charleston, coupled with its Washington arrival at the beginning of the workday on Monday, allowed us to stretch our visit another three hours. From the standpoint of maximizing our time in Charleston, air service would have been a decidedly inferior choice.

And then there is the matter of beholding this country's scenic wonders. Many people are aware of Horseshoe Curve in Pennsylvania and the miles of Puget Sound and Pacific Coast shoreline seen from Amtrak's windows. Other favorite experiences of this author include glimpsing Lake Erie at Sandusky Bay and admiring the splendor of glacier-formed Wisconsin Dells. For memorable Amtrak stopovers, it is difficult to top either Glenwood Springs, with its warm mineral water pool beneath the stars in the mountains of Colorado, or remote Essex, Montana, where one can commune with nature in a bucolic setting far from urban din. And, following a train ride along the peaceful Lake Champlain shore to Port Kent, New York, a ferry takes travelers to Burlington and summer theater on the University of Vermont campus. Descending after dark into the Great Salt Lake Valley or passing the fiery steel mills in Northern Indiana are awe-inspiring experiences. For a reminder of the great river commerce of this nation, we can watch the endless stream of towboats pushing their barges on the Upper Mississippi. And on and on....

Postscript

The following story was recently circulating in multiple venues around the country. It is repeated here to help readers who may not have heard it form their own conclusions relative to the effectiveness of our governmental processes in fostering rail passenger service.

In mid-1996, Amtrak's board of directors considered eliminating the Chicago-Los Angeles Texas Eagle as an economy move in the face of the administration's refusal to budget funds sufficient to sustain the national network. A Dallas couple, who had regularly patronized the train to visit their out-of-state grandchildren and who were precluded from using alternate forms of transportation because of physical impairments, pleaded the train's case in a letter to Vice-President Albert A. Gore, Jr. Here is the vice-president's response:

> Thank you for your letter regarding the protection of the Texas eagle. I share your view that the urgent problem of species extinction and the conservation of biological diversity should be addressed. The first step in saving any plant or animal...is to become aware of and respect the fragile ecosystems that make up our environment.... I look forward to working with you for the future of our planet.

Index

Aeronautical Research Foundation 14-16, 19
Afternoon Hiawatha, The 11
Air Transport Association 60
Airport and Airway Trust Fund 61
Ak-Sar-Ben Zephyr, The 109
Akron Beacon Journal 99
Ambassador, The 103
American Railway Engineering Association 13
Amtrak Improvement Act of 1972 .... 36, 37
Amtrak Improvement Act of 1973 .... 38, 40, 41
Amtrak Improvement Act of 1974 44
Amtrak Improvement Act of 1975 .... 36, 74
Amtrak Improvement Act of 1978 46
Amtrak Reauthorization and Improvement Act of 1990 50
Amtrak 90: A Route to Success 101
Anderson, Jack 60
Ann Arbor Railroad 3
Antelope, The 110
Aquarena Springs, Texas 46
Archives of Environmental Health 66
Argonaut, The 111
Argosy 12
Armstrong, Senator William L. 85
Arrowhead, The 91
Association of American Railroads 14, 19, 27, 38
Atchison, Topeka and Santa Fe Railway 5, 11, 28, 45, 109, 110, 112, 117, 120, 163
Atlanta Journal-Constitution 69
Auto Train Corporation 35, 104
Aztec Eagle, The 44, 45
Badger, The 91
Baltimore and Ohio Railroad 28, 41-43, 67, 89, 97, 103, 105, 107, 122
Baltimore Sun 66
Barriger, John W. 115, 120
Beech Grove Shop, Indiana 37
Berge, Professor Stanley 10, 11, 122
Biden, Senator Joseph R. 86
Biltmore Hotel, Los Angeles 99
Blue Bird, The 11
Blue Ridge, The 41-43
Blue Water, The 77
Boston Globe 66, 73
Bowie Race Track, Maryland 14
Boyd, Alan S. 104
Brinegar, Department of Transportation Secretary Claude S. 38
Broadway Limited, The 36, 41, 48, 54, 55, 97
Budd Company, The 3, 4
Budget of the United States Government 61
Bureau of the Census 22, 82
Burlington Northern Inc. 27, 33, 108, 109, 120, 162
Business World 4
Butte Special, The 19
Byrd, Senator Robert C. 53

California Zephyr, The 11, 35, 52, 112, 120
Canadian National Railways 13, 14
Canadian Pacific Railway 34
Capitol Limited, The 11, 54, 55, 90, 130
Cardinal, The 49, 116, 121
Carolina Special, The 107
Cascade Coast, The 35
Centennial State, The 110
Central Vermont Railway 35
Champion, The 49
Charleston Post and Courier 92
Cher.. 59
Chesapeake and Ohio Railway 14, 28, 42, 66, 67, 108
Chicago Tribune 87
Chicago and North Western Railway 13, 61, 113
Chicago, Burlington and Quincy Railroad 14, 20, 109, 110
Chicago, Milwaukee, St. Paul and Pacific Railroad 13, 33
Chicago, Rock Island and Pacific Railroad 1-3, 34, 40, 62, 109
City of New Orleans, The 35, 161
Civil Aeronautics Administration 17
Civil Aeronautics Board 23, 63, 75
Claytor, W. Graham, Jr. 62
Cleveland Plain Dealer 69, 87
Coast Daylight, The 23, 24
Coast Starlight, The 38, 100, 111, 162
Coaster, The 23
Coefficient of Determination 16
Colorado Eagle, The 11
Columbus Dispatch 99
Commodore Vanderbilt, The 13
Congressional Budget Office 61
Consolidated Rail Corporation 104, 106
Continental Trailways 74-77
Corn Belt Rocket, The 11
Cornell University 66
Coston, James E. 61
Coverdale & Colpitts 3, 4, 11, 12
Crescent, The 62, 63, 69
CSX Transportation, Inc. 103, 106, 108, 121
D'Amato, Senator Alfonse M. 86
Dallas Morning News 91
Danforth, Senator John C. 85
Delaware, Lackawanna and Western Railroad 62
Denver and Rio Grande Western Railroad 2, 34, 110
Denver Post 60, 65
Denver Zephyr, The 20
Department of Defense 5, 6
Department of Transportation 27, 30, 33, 36, 37, 38, 41, 43, 46-50,
                                                                              56-59, 78, 81, 84, 86, 115, 123, 126
Des Moines Rocket, The 11
Desert Wind, The 51, 93
Downs, Thomas M. 129
Durenberger, Senator Dave 86
Empire Builder, The 35, 51, 81, 91, 97, 109
Empire State Express, The.. 40
Environment and Behavior 66
Erie Railroad 13, 14, 97
Fair Labor Standards Act 6

Federal Aviation Administration 47, 60, 61, 65, 67-69, 94, 123
Federal Railroad Administration 27, 36, 44
Floridian, The 35, 49, 89, 121, 161
Fortune 12
French Lick Springs Resort, Indiana 97
Fripp Island Resort, South Carolina 98
General Accounting Office 48, 50, 56, 67, 83-85, 101
General Electric Company 3
General Services Administration 19
George Washington, The.. 11, 42, 66, 67, 90
George Washington University 66
Georgia Railroad 34
Gillespie, Thomas J., Jr. 123
Golden State, The 3, 110
Gopher, The 91
Gore, Vice-President Albert A. Jr. 166
Gould Lines 2
Grand Trunk Western Railroad 33, 113
Great Depression 17
Great Northern Railway 20, 21, 28, 81, 97, 109
Greensboro News & Record 69
Greyhound Lines 23, 58, 79, 82
Gulf Breeze, The 121
Hansbury, John E. 8, 10
Harvard University 12
Harpers Ferry National Park, West Virginia 43, 105
Harwood, Richard 130
Highway Trust Fund 57
Hill, James J. 2
Hilltopper, The 49
Hilton, Professor George W. 81-83, 85
Hosmer, ICC Examiner Howard 20
Houston Chronicle 56, 63
Humming Bird, The 11
I.C.C. Practitioners' Journal 8
Illinois Central Gulf Railroad 36, 40
Illinois Central Railroad 14, 28, 122
Imperial, The 26
Indian Trails, Inc. 77
Inter-American, The 35, 36, 44, 45, 48
Internal Revenue Service 29
International, The 77
International Railway Traveler 124
Interstate Commerce Act, Section 13a 8, 24-26, 62, 104
Interstate Commerce Commission 2, 5-8, 10-17, 19-21, 23-30, 32-36, 38-40,
 46, 47, 62, 79, 82, 83, 104, 116, 122, 126
Itzkoff, Donald M. 17
James Whitcomb Riley, The 35
Journal of Commerce 109
Journal of Personality and Social Psychology 66
Kansas City-Florida Special, The... 11
Kansas City Southern Railway 111
Kansas City Star... 69
Kasich, Representative John R. 57
Kendall, David W. 33
Kendrick, J.W. 1
Kentucky Derby 90
Ladd, Professor Dwight R. 12-14
Lake Shore Limited, The 49, 55, 90, 162

169

Landers, Ann 65
Lark, The 11, 23
Lavin, Christine 59
Least Squares Regression Formula 15
Lewis, Department of Transportation Secretary Drew 104
Lone Star, The 49, 94
Los Angeles Times 99, 129
Louisville and Nashville Railroad 97, 107, 108, 121, 122
Madden, John 59
Magnuson, Senator Warren G. 27
Mainstreeter, The 27
Mall of America, Minnesota 91
Mammoth Cave National Park, Kentucky 97
Marsh, E.S. 11
Mathews, Jessica 53
McCarthy, Colman 56
Meteor, The.. 60
Metroliner, The 39, 80
Metrolink 99, 112
Metropolitan Special, The 107
Missouri-Kansas-Texas Railroad 45
Missouri Pacific Railroad 2, 25, 28, 43-46
Missouri River Eagle, The 11
Mitchell, ICC Chairman Richard F. 11
Modern Railroads 99
Monon Railroad 97
Montréaler, The 35, 49
Morning Daylight, The 11
Motor City Special, The 106
Mount Ranier, The 49
Mule, The 51, 100
Mulvey, Professor Frank P. 77-80, 123
Nancy Hanks II, The 11
National Arbitration Panel 40
National Association of Motor Bus Owners 74, 78
National Association of Railroad and Utilities Commissioners 4-8, 27
National Association of Railroad Passengers 27
National Coal Association 19
National Highway Traffic Safety Administration 56
National Limited, The 41, 43, 45, 49, 67
National Railways of Mexico 44
National Park Service 94
National Transportation Policy Study Commission 77
National Transportation Safety Board 69
National Weather Service 67
Nebraska Zephyr, The... 11
Nelson, Professor James C. 16
New Mexico State University 101
New York Central Railroad 13, 21, 106
New York Daily News 59
New York, New Haven and Hartford Railroad 7, 14
New York Times 57, 129
New York University 66
Newsweek 17
Nixon, President Richard M. 30, 88
Noon Daylight, The 111
Norfolk and Western Railway 113

Norfolk Southern Corporation 103, 108
North American Free Trade Agreement 56
North Coast Hiawatha, The 49, 91
North Coast Limited, The 27
North Star, The 91
Northeastern University 77
Northern Pacific Ry 2, 23, 27, 97, 109
Northwestern Pacific Railroad 113
Northwestern University 10
Official Guide of the Railways 1, 3, 129
Official Register of Passenger Train Equipment 23
Ohio Rail Development Commission 99
Ohio Turnpike 53
Orient Express, The 99
Orr, Governor Robert D. 131
Owl, The 62
Pacemaker, The 13
Pacific International, The 49
Palmetto, The 55, 92, 93
Palmland, The 107
Pan-American, The 90
Passenger Train Journal 80
Peach Queen, The 26
Penn Central Transportation Company 33-37, 40, 42, 67, 103-105
Pennsylvania Railroad 14, 22, 81, 97, 104
Pennsylvanian, The 94
Peoria Rocket, The 11
Perot, Ross 91
Philadelphia Inquirer 66
Pioneer, The 36, 49, 51, 86, 161
Popular Science 4
Portland Oregonian 62
Post Office Department 5, 25
Potomac Special, The 41
Potomac River 55, 65, 71
Pullman Company, The 17-20, 90, 130, 162
Pullman-Standard Car Manufacturing Company 16
Quaker, The 14
Rail Passenger Service Act of 1970 .... 30, 79, 80
Rail Travel News 130
Railway Age 11, 23, 86, 100
Railway Express Agency 6
Railway Labor Executives' Association 20, 27
Railway Post Office 25
Railway Progress Institute 16
Ray, Governor Dixie Lee 47
Reistrup, Paul H. 85
Rock and Roll Hall of Fame and Museum, Ohio 90
Rocky Mountain Rocket, The 11
Roncalio, Representative Teno 47
Roosevelt Memorial 65
Roth, Senator William V., Jr. 57
Russell's Official National Motor Coach Guide 58, 79
Rutland Railroad 13
San Francisco Chief, The 112
San Francisco Examiner 100
San Francisco Zephyr, The 47, 49
San Joaquin, The 49

Seaboard Coast Line Railroad 14, 28, 107, 121, 122
Shasta Daylight, The 26
Sheck, Professor Ronald C. 101, 102, 114, 116
Shenandoah, The 128
Silver Comet, The 107
Silver Meteor, The 11, 49, 93, 162, 164
Silver Palm, The 93
Silver Star, The 55
Simpson, O.J. 93
Slattery, Representative Jim 130, 131
Slumbercoach 20, 128
South Wind, The 35, 90
Southern Belle, The 111
Southern Crescent, The 49, 79, 89
Southern Pacific Company 2, 3, 13, 14, 22-24, 26, 111
Southern Railway 26, 28, 34, 62, 89, 107, 122
Southerner, The 11
Southwest Chief, The 93, 109, 115-120
Southwest Limited, The 48
Spector, Senator Arlen 86
"Spirit of St. Louis," The 67
Spoleto Festival 93
Sportsman, The 66
St. Louis Post-Dispatch 60, 100, 128
St. Louis-San Francisco Railway 60, 108, 122
St. Louis Southwestern Railway 45, 110
Stafford, ICC Chairman George M. 32
Staggers, Representative Harley O. 27, 41
Stanford Research Institute 22-24, 126
Sunnyland, The 108
Sunset Limited, The 3, 51, 92, 94, 96, 111, 121, 164
Sunshine Special, The 44
Super Chief, The 35
Susquehanna River 33
Talgo Train 20
Tennessean, The 11
Terminal Railroad Association of St. Louis 36
Texas and Pacific Railway 25, 35, 40, 46
Texas Chief, The 35, 44
Texas Eagle, The 44, 56, 92, 94, 96, 110, 166
Texas Special, The 60
Texas Zephyr, The 110
Thomas Cook, Ltd. 124
Thosteson, George C., M.D. 69
Three Rivers, The 54
Tierney, ICC Chairman Paul J. 27
Traffic World 109, 129
Trailways Bus 58
Train X 20
Trains 127
Transportation Association of America 57
Transportation Facts, Inc. 16
Turbo Train 36, 41
Twilight Limited, The 83-85, 120
Twin Star Rocket, The 11
Twin Zephyrs, The 11
United States Railway Association 33
Union Pacific Railroad 19, 28, 45, 110, 112

University of Arizona 164
University of California 66, 81
University of Idaho 81
University of Maryland 89
University of Minnesota 89
University of Oregon 66
University of South Florida 101
University of Vermont 165
University of Western Ontario 12
USA Today 129
VIA Rail Canada 105, 106, 109
Volpe, Department of Transportation Secretary John A. 30
Wabash Railroad 113
Wall Street Journal 62, 68, 98, 100, 130
Wallop, Senator Malcolm 85
Washington Post 53, 55, 56, 58, 59, 61, 65, 67, 68, 71, 72, 88, 91, 93, 129, 130
Washington Star 66
Washington State University 16
Washington Terminal Company 42
Western Pacific Railroad 2
Western Star, The 28
Who's Who in America 115
Williams, Ted 73
Wilner, Frank N. 127
Wolverine, The 120
World Health Organization 70
World War II 5, 17, 20, 21, 157
Wyer, Dick & Co. 27
Xplorer Train 20
Yager Formula 13
Yale University 14
Young, Dick 59